D1240264

PREACHING
IN AN AGE OF
DISTRACTION

J. ELLSWORTH KALAS

IVP Books

An imprint of InterVarsity Press
Downers Grove, Illinois

InterVarsity Press
P.O. Box 1400, Downers Grove, IL 60515-1426
World Wide Web: www.ivpress.com
Email: email@ivpress.com

InterVarsity Press® is the book-publishing division of InterVarsity Christian Fellowship/USA®, a movement of students and faculty active on campus at hundreds of universities, colleges and schools of nursing in the United States of America, and a member movement of the International Fellowship of Evangelical Students. For information about local and regional activities, write Public Relations Dept., InterVarsity Christian Fellowship/USA, 6400 Schroeder Rd., P.O. Box 7895, Madison, WI 53707-7895, or visit the IVCF website at www.intervarsity.org.

All Scripture quotations, unless otherwise indicated, are taken from the Common English Bible (CEB). © 2011 *by* Common English Bible.

While all stories in this book are true, some names and identifying information in this book have been changed to protect the privacy of the individuals involved.

Cover design: David Fassett
Interior design: Beth Hagenberg
Images: communication icons: © Step_Pe/iStockphoto;
  graphic elements and icons: © -Mosquito-/iStockphoto;
  graphic symbols: © artvea/iStockphoto

ISBN 978-0-8308-4110-3 (print)
ISBN 978-0-8308-7966-3 (digital)

Printed in the United States of America ∞

Library of Congress Cataloging-in-Publication Data
A catalog record for this book is available from the Library of Congress.

P	21	20	19	18	17	16	15	14	13	12	11	10	9	8	7	6	5	4	3	2	1
Y	31	30	29	28	27	26	25	24	23	22	21	20	19	18	17	16	15	14			

True friends are a divine gift at all times but particularly so in times of complex need. Years ago, at such a time in my life, God blessed me with two such friends, Malcolm McCuaig (now with his Lord) and Maxie Dunnam.

I dedicate this book to them with a sense of eternal gratitude.

CONTENTS

1

PREACHING IN AN
AGE OF DISTRACTION

I have pursued the art, craft and calling of preaching since the middle of the last century and I still thank God daily—yes, sometimes several times a day—for the privilege of standing in a pulpit or its equivalent. For me there is no higher calling. I'd like to give another life to it.

But I know that starting again in this second decade of the twenty-first century would be very different from the world in which I began preaching, or even the world of a decade or two ago. We live in the Age of Distraction, and it seems to be accelerating.

Not that distraction is new to me as a preacher. It comes with the territory. I didn't realize it at the time, but sometimes during my teenage years I was myself a distraction to the preacher and to some of the people sitting nearby. Crying babies and happy, playful infants have always been a challenge in churches without a nursery room. I think back often on those loyal dairy farmers who had been up before dawn to do their chores. Now, in the warmth of the church and with the preacher's voice drifting comfortably over them, they fell asleep during the sermon. For a time this distracted me terribly, but I slowly realized that their happy rest didn't bother anyone else and it shouldn't bother me.

Along the way there were occasions of dramatic distraction. I still shiver slightly when I recall the bat that visited our worship service one Sunday morning, swooping down repeatedly while I tried to hold a dodging congregation attentive to the sermon. And there was the Good Friday service during the Vietnam War when six or eight university students stood up midway through a sermon and unfurled banners challenging the war. They remained standing for the rest of the message.

But it's a different ball game today. I sense it when I stand up to preach, as I do fifty or sixty times a year, or as I listen to friends who are every-Sunday preachers. It's not just the prospect of a cell phone ringing during a sermon. Most people have learned to turn off the sound before coming to church. Some even leave the cell phone in the car. But it's not as easy to leave the cell phone mentality in the car. We've developed a kind of mental and emotional edginess that goes with us even when the materials of implementation are not there.

Phrases of the culture say as much. We belong to the "always-on, always-connected digital world," and we find it gratifying to see ourselves that way. Many of the people who come to church on Sunday have just watched a sitcom the night before, with its changing scene every ten or fifteen seconds and its three or four commercials in the space of a minute. Can we expect people who experience life in such fashion all through the week to give undivided attention to a sermon or a prayer when they're accustomed to living with several clamoring voices surrounding them at all times?

The psalm tells us, "Be still, and know that I am God" (Ps 46:10 NRSV). Our worshipers answer, "The quiet makes me nervous."

For Preachers and Teachers, a Double Problem

Distractions present a double peril for us preachers and teachers. As communicators we have to find ways to hold the attention of people who live in the world of distractions. But we have minds and souls of our own: minds that are supposed to be creative and souls that are supposed to be God-centered. As we seek these ends we cope with distractions and intrusions in our study and devotional time that our pulpit ancestors could never have imagined.

But of course distractions aren't unique to the twentieth and twenty-first centuries. They didn't begin with the Internet or with television or radio. They're as old as the Garden of Eden. Distraction wasn't the original sin, but it opened the door for it. Nor is distraction simply another name for temptation, but temptation surely finds a primary ally in distraction.

Let's look at the Eden story for a moment to put twenty-first-century distractions in theological perspective. Adam and Eve didn't get into trouble because Eden was boring. They had plenty to occupy their minds and talents. One another, to begin with. Whether they knew it or not, when they looked at each other they saw the basic plot for every short story, novel and drama that would ever be written and quite a bit of the poetry as well. And of course there was plenty to explore in their own persons. One doesn't have to be a narcissist to find one's self unceasingly interesting and surprising.

Adam and Eve had work to do, too, as resident managers of an enterprise called perfection. The varieties of the creation around them were so enchanting and so complex that millennia later their descendants are still exploring the territory. This work assignment could itself have claimed their full attention without ever coming to an end of wonders and confusions.

But most of all, there was God. Here was the one around whom all the other issues and interests—self, work, companions, nature, whatever—revolved and in whom they found their purpose and glory. To be right with God was to be right with all else, and seeing all else through the prism of God's purposes was to see all else properly and to relate with it harmoniously. It was not that any of these other factors were bad or that they were not important. Quite the contrary; as part of God's plan, they had singular importance. But the wonder was to know God, to sense the pleasure that God finds in us. Nothing could compare with this.

So it seems that Adam and Eve didn't really need anything. Nevertheless, they got distracted. An intruder got them thinking about other things. As it happened, this thinking led to an act of disobedience, but it began with a diversion of attention. And as the rule of learning reminds us, what gets our attention gets us.

What gets our attention isn't necessarily bad. But neither, unfortunately, is it necessarily important, worthy or admirable. Nor is it necessarily lasting. Indeed, it sometimes seems that the more transient and insubstantial a matter is, the more easily it engages and distracts us. It's as if the mind and soul are inclined to be lazy and therefore to reach first for the low-hanging fruit. Perhaps it's because we've trained ourselves that way. Children, by contrast, show a remarkable capacity for the profound. So it is that they ask questions we adults push aside, not because the questions are unimportant but because they are so basic and therefore so difficult. In time, most children stop asking such questions and settle for talking about what is transient and therefore manageable. That is, they too learn to reach for the low-hanging fruit.

So we humans seem to have a penchant for distraction. And here's where the problem gets complicated. Because, you see, distraction is not altogether bad. In many ways distraction is our learning edge. Distraction fuels our instinct for exploration. It could be argued that every invention, good or evil, begins with distraction, with seeing things that might be different and that therefore might also be better, or at least more interesting. Unfortunately, however, our inclination to distraction lacks good taste except as by God's grace it is transformed. It is to the degree that we cooperate with God in refining our taste that our minds are drawn more to that which is worthy, beautiful, productive and redemptive.

The Seductive Power of Distraction

But this isn't easy. Most of us have discovered while in an airplane, on a bus or on a subway that something perverse in our makeup finds more attraction in that which is not our business, or at least not our primary business, than in what we should be attending to. When I travel I bring with me material that I really want to read, either because it is important to my life and work or simply because its subject matter fascinates me. I know that my proposed travel reading should be commanding in its own right, so I choose it carefully. Nevertheless, if the person sitting next to me pulls out a book or a periodical, I can't resist sneaking a look. Sometimes I'll read along for a page or more, often stopped only by the fear that the person next to me will sense that I'm snooping. Unfortunately, distraction feeds on itself so that the distraction that could conceivably lead to exploration and invention often breeds, instead, simply more distraction.

Consider, too, the nearby person with a cell phone. We don't really care about this stranger's business or personal affairs but we can hardly resist listening. Veronica V. Galvan, an assistant professor of psychology at the University of San Diego, has been part of an academic study that shows that overheard telephone conversations "are far more distracting and annoying than a dialogue between two people nearby." Why? Psychologists have determined that it is "the brain's desire to fill in the blanks; we're troubled by what is now called a 'half-a-logue.'"[1]

Some think that we are part of the most distracted generation in human history. I'm constitutionally uneasy about using words like "the most," "the least," "the worst" or "the best," because I know just enough history to realize that it's hard to prove such superlatives. Even so, I can't help feeling that whether or not distraction is now at its worst, it is certainly at a level where it imposes serious hazards to what is best in our human character, and it presents particular issues to those of us who try to lead by preaching, teaching and writing.

First, however, let me put the issue in perspective by looking briefly at other times and cultures. The book of Proverbs doesn't speak directly of distractions, but the inference is there in all of the book's passionate appeals for wisdom. The first word after the prologue is "Listen" (Prov 1:8). This is the teacher or parent insisting that we put aside all distractions. And again, "Hear, children . . . pay attention" (Prov 4:1). "Focus your eyes straight ahead; / keep your gaze on what is in front of you" (Prov 4:25)—that is, don't let anything distract you. "My son, pay attention to my wisdom. / Bend your ear to what I know" (Prov 5:1). It sounds as if the ancient Hebrew parent-teacher struggled as much with distracted listeners as any of us twenty-first-century advocates. The biblical writers knew that wisdom comes only to those whose attention is intense and that the greatest hazard to wisdom begins with inattention—that is, by distraction.

Distraction uses some of our best powers. Take memory, for in-

Not sure all th's, is "distraction"

stance. Memory is a priceless gift, but memory is also an entry point for distraction. The infant nation of Israel was hardly out of captivity and was in need of full attention to face the challenges of its new role when it became distracted by memories: specifically, the memory of Egypt and its varieties of food. This, of course, led to complaining, which is the opposite of faith, and Israel was in trouble. When Moses was on Sinai receiving the Law that would guide the new nation, the people were distracted by his absence and then by the memory of gods they had seen others worship, visible gods, so with Aaron's help they made a golden calf. Memory, that lovely ally in living, also assists distraction.

And of course our neighbors can give aid to distraction. This is true not only in the material the person beside us is reading or in what the person at the next table at the restaurant ordered but in much larger matters. In Samuel's day the people were distracted by the form of government they saw in their neighboring nations and decided that they, too, should have a king. In generation after generation the perceived prosperity of such neighbors distracted Israel from the Lord God, making them wonder if Baal might be better. Thus envy lent its power to distraction.

Perhaps it's no exaggeration to say that the Hebrew prophets came into existence to deal with Israel's tendency toward distraction. Thus Isaiah, in God's stead, reminded the people that the ox and the donkey, simple as they were, nevertheless knew their owner and their master's crib, but God's people, Israel, a "sinful nation," didn't know the Lord God who had watched over them from their birth as a nation. Let's say the ox and the donkey were better focused. But of course that's easy for them because they aren't as complex as we are. Amos denounced those who were so distracted by prosperity and self-indulgence that they could no longer see the needs of the poor.

Haggai preached to a people with whom we might secretly sympathize: they were so preoccupied with paneling their own homes that they forgot that the house of the Lord was in ruins. All of which is to say, distraction comes easily, in many forms, and it happens to the nicest people.

Distractions Keep Speeding Up

We complain in the twenty-first century that the speed of living distracts us, and there's plenty of evidence to make the case. But Thomas De Quincey found it so in 1849 as he indicated in his essay "The English Mail-Coach." The mail had gained "velocity," and so too did those who traveled in the mail coach: "We find ourselves in York four hours after leaving London." The world was speeding up for De Quincey. But he found that it was at a price. The traveler who idled along on horseback saw the fox and her kittens and caught the scent of roadside flowers or newly mown hay. There was time even to exchange greetings with walkers or with other horseback riders. Now De Quincey was losing those benefits of the slower world.

Yet even as I read De Quincey's essay, I find myself wanting to hasten the author's pace. He had more time to play with words and more time for the idle pleasure of gentle humor than we're accustomed to. There is beauty in the language and a certain gentility in the unhurried pace, but a contemporary reader may get uneasy with ambling along or even find it tedious. We expect our sentences to be airplane-fast or at least test the interstate speed limit; we're not comfortable with the speed of the mail coach, to say nothing of the wanderer on horseback. We are so accustomed to being hurried and distracted that we hardly know how to read at De Quincey's pace or Samuel Johnson's or Montaigne's. And goodness knows that text messaging isn't making it any better.

Advertising hurries our life, but more than that it complicates it. It has become ever-present. In the process it can easily make our generation feel that our main purpose in living is to be consumers; indeed, that if we don't keep grasping after what is new and enticing and probably expensive, the economic structure of the Western world will collapse. No doubt this is worse in our day, but William Wordsworth felt it more than two hundred years ago when he wrote, "The world is too much with us; late and soon, / Getting and spending, we lay waste our powers."

So we humans have always had a problem. Distraction is our middle name. If it is true, as the book of Job so famously puts it, that we are "born to trouble just as sparks fly upward" (Job 5:7 NRSV), it seems that our inclination to distraction blows on those sparks. Even so, distraction is not all bad. After all, any voice that solicits our attention by seeking to draw our attention away from sin or self-centeredness or from that which is harmful to ourselves or others is itself a form of distraction. But it is a redemptive form. Life moves, for both good and ill, by its attractions and distractions.

So here's the problem. You and I live in a time when distraction has taken on a life of its own. Its powers have become so sophisticated that much of the time we don't even realize it is at work in us and on us. Some of the most creative and imaginative minds in our culture have a full-time assignment to get our attention and to move it away from other matters. Some of these bright minds are in advertising. Consider that football's Super Bowl is not only the largest television spectacle of the year, it is also the most expensive and persuasive conglomerate of commercials. These commercials are developed to be so attractive that members of some households who are not sports fans stay tuned just to see the commercials.

But before a manufacturer brings the product to an advertising agency, he has employed experts in the field of packaging. These counselors want to wrap the product so it will distract shoppers from all the other containers in that section of the store. Other experts have spent hundreds of hours concocting a name for the product, in hopes that the name will offend few and enchant many. And somewhere prior to all of this investment in genius, students of public opinion have estimated whether there is a market for this particular product at this time in economic history, because if no market exists, even the best of distractions may fail. Perhaps we can be forgiven if we envy our spiritual ancestors in Eden. They had to worry about only one tree. For us, Distraction is the name of the forest.

If you get the feeling that you and I are nearly helpless in the face of such a world, you may be right. Perhaps not you, personally, because you're a reader and as a reader you are inclined to give more time to decision making. That is, you are not as easily seduced by every vagrant voice. But none of us is immune to the appeal, and sometimes our very feeling of distance and superiority only makes us more susceptible to what is happening in some corners of our souls. More than that, all of us have to deal with the fallout of this world of distraction. The daily press, radio, television, Internet—we are all atwitter whether or not we personally tweet. And those who are most captive to distraction are often those with whom we live and converse. What we avoid by intention gets at us secondhand.

Those of us who preach, teach or write are in constant battle on the field of distractions. We are engaged in the struggle for the souls of humankind: we compete daily for their time, their attention, their feelings and eventually their commitment and conduct. For us, distraction is not just a personal problem with which we, like the rest of our race, must contend. It is much more; because of our calling and because of the talents we hope we possess, we must enter the distraction competition. We're not satisfied that the race should go by default to those who have the largest budgets, the best polling data or the most sophisticated facilities. We feel compelled to make our case because we believe that, quite simply, it must be made.

If that be so, we must learn how to be heard and to be heard persuasively. It is not acceptable to complain about the times or bemoan the problems. If distraction is a fact of our era, then we are called as faith-communicators to contend with it. If, further, distraction is a dominant factor in our times, we should waste no time in knowing how to use it rather than allowing it to make us irrelevant.

Fortunately, we're not alone in this battle. God, who has chosen to "discern my thoughts from far away" and who is "acquainted with all my ways" (Ps 139:2-3 NRSV) is not undone by our world of distractions. By our relationship with God, we are ready to meet whatever distractions may come our way and the way of the people whom we serve.

MANY THINGS . . . ONE THING

While distractions have been an issue for people of faith in every age, our era seems especially prone to distraction. As Kalas notes, television commercials have turned distraction into an industry. Each of these fifteen-second to one-minute segments is designed to distract us from whatever else we are doing, thinking or feeling. The goal is to entice us to focus instead on their product, which is sure to change our lives for the better.

While these and other modern distractions quickly wear thin, they also wear us out. We are left exhausted and unfulfilled by the persistence of life's distractions. After a long day in the kitchen, Martha complained that while she had been bending over backward to provide radical hospitality for Jesus, her sister had been content simply to sit at Jesus' feet and listen to his teaching and reflections.

Instead of complimenting Martha for her hard work and dedication, Jesus rebukes her: "Martha, you are worried and distracted by many things" (Lk 10:41). Was Jesus talking to Martha, or is he talking to us as we try to multitask our way through life? "One thing is necessary," Jesus continues (Lk 10:42). What one thing do we need to focus on in our preaching? Isn't the "one thing" clearly to communicate the timeless message of the gospel in the ever-changing and constantly distracting environment in which we find ourselves? Amidst all the distractions of twenty-first-century life, may God give us the courage and the fortitude to "keep the main thing the main thing."

Charles Yoost, senior minister, Church of the Saviour, Cleveland Heights, Ohio

2

NAMING AN AGE

I suspect that every generation has been impressed with its own significance to the point of naming itself. The book of Genesis suggests it early with its report on the descendants of Cain, particularly the boasting of Lamech and the achievements of his sons (Gen 4:17-24). It sounds as if they saw themselves as the age of progress. History shows that some generations have in truth been special, and they've had writers or speakers who found a phrase to describe it. Thomas Paine saw the period of the American Revolution as "the times that try men's souls." When Franklin Delano Roosevelt sought a second term in office he challenged his hearers to see themselves as a generation that had "a rendezvous with destiny." When Martin Luther King Jr. declared his dream, it was an implicit appeal to others to join him in becoming an age of dreamers.

Obviously we have no idea of the age-naming that has proven presumptuous or ridiculous. The worst that can be said about our time is that we've gone overboard. With the help of psychologists, social scientists and not a few astute publicists, we have divided the population into neat communities to whom we've given names—Boomers,

Gen-Xers, Millennials and so on. We have then ordained that people in any particular subset have certain buying, eating, entertaining and spiritual instincts. If some sensitive person discovers that he belongs chronologically to the Boomers but doesn't reflect their profile, does he feel like a sociological variation on Edward Everett Hale's short story "The Man Without a Country," doomed forever to travel from one rejecting port after another, or like Tom Hanks's stateless character wandering through the airport in *The Terminal*? I hope not, but I wouldn't be surprised if this were the case. Such is the price of living in a name-giving era.

Nevertheless, it's clear that there are times and seasons in our human story and that sometimes they vary distinctively enough that we understand ourselves and our history better when we recognize the distinctions. And even if at times we trivialize the boundaries by exaggerated or misdirected attention, they help us understand the times in which we live and perhaps help us live in them more effectively.

The apostle Paul said as much when he appealed to the believers in Rome, saying, "Don't be conformed to the patterns of this world, but be transformed by the renewing of your minds so that you can figure out what God's will is—what is good and pleasing and mature" (Rom 12:2). Paul knew that his converts needed to understand their times if they were to grasp the distinction between "the patterns of this world"—that is, the culture of their times—and the eternal purposes of God. I suspect that one of the most serious problems of the average contemporary believer is that we are so at home in our culture that we don't bother to analyze it or to ask ourselves how its patterns compare to the purposes of God. Jesus condemned the Pharisees and Sadducees for their inability to "recognize the signs that point to what the time is" (Mt 16:3).

So yes: those of us who intend to speak to our times must seek to understand the times in which we live. We need, of course, to be careful that we aren't carried away with each new public opinion survey or the latest entertainment fad. And in a world like ours (that is, a world of distractions), it's nearly impossible to keep up with such changes and to estimate their relative importance. Look at a periodical that you laid aside two years ago and see how much of it is still worth reading today. Ponder how some persons and issues that were then in vogue are now obscure if not forgotten.

Some things, however, are significant. Some will be an issue for a whole generation. More than that, some will pick up speed and power as time unfolds so that they become even more significant for our children and grandchildren than they are now to us. And in some instances, if we don't deal redemptively with these elements now, the effect on future generations will be harmful beyond our imagining.

It is in this mood and with this sense of responsibility that I urge us to think of our time as the Age of Distraction and to consider our role as communicators in such a time. I'm sure I'm not the first person to give this name to our culture and certainly, whatever the name, I'm not the only one to feel frustrated by this characteristic of our time and the power it holds over us. It's worth naming the time, because—in the mood of the Rumpelstiltskin theory—if we can name a thing we can prevent its controlling us.

Distraction is not unique to our times. We humans have always been susceptible to matters other than the ones that should have a primary claim on our attention. Robert Louis Stevenson said that "the world is so full of a number of things, I'm sure we should all be as happy as kings." This world is indeed "full of a number of things." God has created it with such abundance and variety that we humans will never come to an end of our exploring. So this curiosity of ours that leads to distraction is part of our genetic code. We are the designated explorers in God's creation, and our call to explore, along with our ability to do so, is one of our greatest gifts from God.

At the same time, however, unless we channel our curiosity, we become like Stephen Leacock's rider who "flung himself upon his horse and rode madly off in all directions." Our curiosity, even if we call it our desire to learn, is of little value until we help it to concentrate. Distraction is the name we give to curiosity gone to no purpose, a thief of time and mind in a world of riches. And distraction has powers in our age, I dare to say, beyond any time in previous generations. At this point I can hardly imagine distraction growing still more insistent and more seductive, but almost surely it will be a greater hazard for our children than it is for us. There seems no reason to expect its powers to diminish.

The Distracting Marketplace

Let's start with the confusion of choices that challenges us on even the most routine shopping trip. Fifteen years ago a missionary told me of his culture shock when on a furlough in America he went out to buy a box of cereal for his family. He found himself confronted by a variety that both overwhelmed and depressed him. As he spoke, I recalled how the world of breakfast cereals had changed since my rather-long-ago boyhood, when the possibilities in the cooked category were oatmeal or Cream of Wheat, and for cold cereals we had bran flakes, shredded wheat, puffed wheat and corn flakes—and also the somewhat more exotic Grape Nuts and Wheaties (which also provided a picture of an athletic hero). My missionary friend resented that the multiplied possibilities compelled him to invest so much good time in what ought to have been an uncomplicated errand. And because he had been living in a far simpler world, he was somewhat disdainful of our American fascination with something as basic as breakfast cereal.

If the missionary were to make a similar shopping trip today, he would need a statistician's skills to record his feelings. Professor Barry Schwartz says that his neighborhood supermarket isn't particularly large, but he counted 275 varieties of cereal, including 24 oatmeal options alone. And that was only the beginning. He also found 230 soup possibilities, a salad bar with 55 different items, and 285 varieties of cookies with 21 possibilities among chocolate chip cookies.[1] (Whatever happened to Toll House cookies, once the only name in the race?) As I read the professor's report, I thought also of the specialty stores in my city, where people with trained tastes and a penchant for discussing shopping at social gatherings love to do business; in such emporia one can find brands and sub-brands that never appear in the supermarkets.

By now perhaps I'm irritating those who feel I want to rob them of their freedom to shop. Heaven forbid! I'm only suggesting that we need go no farther than our local supermarket, drugstore or specialty shop to see how complex our lives have become—and this at the most commonplace level, our daily bread. We can rightly extrapolate from there that our culture not only is packed full of distractions but that we have come to take most of those distractions for granted, not realizing how much they claim of our time, our attention and our psychic energy. Still worse, I suspect some would argue that it is the very variety of these choices that makes the free enterprise system work.

Some might ask if I want to reduce our culture to a set of drab government-controlled markets or whether I want to live on a same-food-three-times-a-day menu that people know in some parts of the world. I plead earnestly innocent to all such charges. Nevertheless,

I wonder how much of our time we spend choosing between fine print labels and glossy displays. And more than that, I wonder if all of these marginal exercises of choosing distract us from issues of more merit. The wily emperors of ancient Rome decided that they could control the masses by a combination of food and circuses. Today the grocery store is itself a glamour trip and the circus comes on television when we get home. Or if we're in a hurry (as most of us seem to be much of the time), we can get life's circus by way of the apps on our cell phone.

How does such a daily culture affect our sensitivity to issues that are eternal? Do we spend so much emotional and spiritual energy on material choices that we have neither the time nor the inclination to focus our souls on the kingdom that fadeth not? The apostle urged first-century believers, "From now on, brothers and sisters, if anything is excellent and if anything is admirable, focus your thoughts on these things: all that is true, all that is holy, all that is just, all that is pure, all that is lovely, and all that is worthy of praise" (Phil 4:8). If the foods that feed our bodies influence our physical health, certainly the ideas and impressions that crowd their way into our minds help shape and determine our intellectual, emotional and spiritual welfare. That's why we need so badly to focus our thoughts, because otherwise they will be lost in a maze of spiritual waste.

Paul's first-century world had its share of competing voices. Sex and violence were present, just as they are in our culture. In fact, sex had a special venue because some of the pagan religions featured temple prostitutes. Violence had dramatic sway in the spectacles of the coliseums. Sports were a great attraction in the culture that gave us the Olympics. And it was a world full of ideas. The classic Greek philosophers Socrates, Plato and Aristotle were gone, but the fascination with such thinking still pervaded the Roman Empire. And the bazaars, which might seem limited compared to our shopping malls, had a vigor and charm of their own.

But if it was difficult for the saints at Philippi to think on the true, holy, just and lovely, I daresay theirs were the minor leagues of competing thoughts when laid alongside our world. It's true that Paul found Athens a place where "all Athenians as well as the foreigners who live in Athens used to spend their time doing nothing but talking about or listening to the newest thing" (Acts 17:21), but there simply weren't as many "manufacturers" of the new as is the case in our day and certainly nothing to compare with our contemporary sophistication in communicating the new. Fleming Rutledge observes, "It is axiomatic in the advertising industry that the quality of newness itself recommends a product."[2] A familiar product that was already our first choice suddenly bears a label with three magic words: "new and improved." The first word is enough for many, but for those who liked the product as it was, the second word seeks to reassure us. We'll have what we always liked but we'll have more, too; something in it will be new.

In a sense, this is the essence of distraction. It seeks our attention even when we're happy as we are. Distraction insists that the change will be better. So this is your lifelong-favorite cereal? Now we offer you your favorite improved. You say you're completely satisfied with it as it is? How can you be sure until you've tried the improved form? There's something in our culture, serpentlike, that keeps telling us that however satisfied we think we are, something is missing. And there's something in our human makeup that seems to be waiting for just such solicitations.

In our time no altar is as appealing as the altar of the new. You and I can become unintentional, full-time test markets for various expressions of newness. I don't want "new" to become the most seductive word in the English language. Nor do I want our values to be judged on the degree to which we are authorities on what is new. One may have to make a philosophical statement to justify the ancient preacher when he declared that there's nothing new under the sun, but at the least we need to know that there's nothing new of such ultimate significance as to bet our souls on it. And for that reason, the altar of newness is a poor place to bow.

Neither would I give undue time to the whipping horse of materialism. I can't say that I admire the princes of merchandising, but I am somewhat in awe of their ability to reinvent their products in so many forms. But the marketplace is a secondary player in this matter of our distraction. The bigger question has to do with those forces that get us into the marketplace, both appeals from without and urges from within. Still, I can't help noting that after Adam and Eve sinned, they immediately went shopping. And to notice also that they were shopping for a cover-up. I wouldn't develop a doctrine around this observation, but it's worth more than a passing thought.

Entertainment as Distraction

Then there's the world of entertainment. Neil Postman warned us half a generation ago that we were *Amusing Ourselves to Death*. And that was before cable television multiplied the channel options almost exponentially without necessarily improving the general quality. That was before the sports enthusiasts could be assured that they could watch their favorite team no matter and wherever. It was before, indeed, a football fan could enjoy—if that's the right word— having several games on the screen at the same time. Talk about distraction! This provision allows a viewer to observe several games a little bit yet none of them fully, unconsciously en route to frustration.

And this, still more, was before parents began providing their children with a movie in the back seat so that the long trip (or even a trip to the shopping mall) wouldn't be punctuated by, "Are we there yet?" Parents tell me of this provision while they're recalling the fun they themselves experienced collecting the names of states via license plates on other automobiles or alphabet games they manufactured from billboards. And it was before one carried a television set, game board and camera in what is disguised as a telephone.

These are marvels, no doubt about it. But what time do they leave for original thinking? Or for examining one's own soul? And to what degree do these matters frustrate the brain's ability to focus, as Paul put it, on the good, the beautiful, and the true, rather than be controlled by the transient, the trivial and the traumatic? And what are we doing to the coming generation if we crowd their time and attention with artificial intelligence to the diminishing of their own creativity?

Most of us have to confess that we are essentially novices in the matter of entertainment. I enjoy sports and some television and movies and stage plays and music from sacred and classical to country and western. But on those occasions when I read *The New York Times*, I discover that I haven't skimmed the surface. I see full-page advertisements for movies that I didn't know existed. The very size of the ad suggests that I'm missing something I ought to see. And the wonders of ballet, specialized musical venues, experimental off-Broadway drama, art exhibits, poetry readings: How in the world can one keep up with it all?

Sports and Work

Sports have probably had a place in human life for as far back as we have any record. But where once sports offered diversion, now their claim on many has become distraction. Beyond television there are fantasy leagues, where you can build your own team and enjoy the exhilaration and frustration of being manager and owner. At one time sports was for Dad or Mom to play catch with a child or perhaps a game of horse on a garage hoop. Now the aim is to have a child involved in three or four or more sports, starting with very little leagues. Even in grade school many children are involved in several sports at the same time. With such a schedule, families give up another meal at home and eat in the car while going to a game or practice. And if there are several children, one parent can go to basketball with a son while another goes to soccer with a daughter. I'm not quoting statistics, I'm only describing what I observe any day of the week, including Sunday, and reminding you of what you already know—perhaps by painful experience.

And with all of that, most of us work too much. That's the opinion of Matthew Sleeth, a medical doctor and hospital administrator who is now a full-time advocate for God's creation and for restoring the Sabbath into our daily week. He reminds us that in the last twenty years, work is up fifteen percent and leisure time has decreased thirty percent. He describes the common scenario of multitasking and multiple jobs, a world where "Mom works two jobs and so do Dad and Sis." Fifty years ago, he recalls, sociologists were predicting that our future problem would be too much spare time; how would we cope with three-day workweeks and four months of vacation annually? Now life is 24/7.[3] Most of us don't know how it happened and even fewer of us know what to do about it—even in our own lives, let alone in the culture at large.

My aim is to inspire change, not to seed despair. But we won't change until we know we're in trouble, and here's the particular quality of our trouble. While our cultural environment overwhelms us with distractions, there's something inside you and me that seems to encourage it. After years in New York City, Kathleen Norris moved to Lemmon, South Dakota, a town of less than two thousand—fewer people, I venture, than in a square block of Manhattan—and made a discovery: "I was dismayed to find that in a tiny town that offered very little in the way of distraction, I nevertheless managed to be distracted much of the time."[4]

It's as if some evil genie has decided to drive us mad by spreading before us more than we want, more than we can imagine, certainly more than we can contain, and then cursed us with an inability to really enjoy any of it because we won't focus long enough on any one thing to savor its flavor. And if this was a problem for our ancestors, who had to deal with competing thoughts while the only external distraction was the nearby creek, the languid cloud or the chirping bird, how do we manage in a culture where sensory stimuli are literally beyond counting?

Medical and social scientists alike are compiling studies on the effect a distracted lifestyle has on our bodies and minds. We preachers ask a further question: What is happening to our souls? Our desires have become larger than we can manage even as we are stimulated to seek still more. Our mothers and grandmothers had a descriptive phrase when a child (or an undisciplined adult) took too large a helping of food and left a sizeable portion on the plate. "His eyes were bigger than his stomach," they said. This homely phrase may be the best way to describe our contemporary way of life. Our eyes—seduced by the continuing wave of new products, voices that tell us that what we have is no longer enough, the specter of envy reminding us that if our neighbor has something, we must have it too—our eyes see so much that even when our plate of time (to say nothing of checkbook and credit cards) is brimming over the edges, we think we must still get more, see more, hear more, ingest more, crave more.

At this moment someone might ask, "So what difference does it make? What if we spend our time and energy jumping from one excitement to another? Does it matter that these are times of distraction?" Well, it matters if you and I matter. If we see ourselves simply as grazing animals, moving from one excitement to another the way the beast moves from one tuft of grass to the next, then I suspect it doesn't matter. But if we see ourselves as creatures of purpose—and indeed, if we see ourselves as God sees us, as creatures with an eternal purpose—then it matters profoundly.

If our age is the Age of Distraction, there's a unique responsibility for the teacher, the preacher and the thoughtful journalist or essayist. In every age the gospel has had to deal with some pervasive mood or other, whether doubt, anger, scorn or apathy. But at least those moods compelled us to face life's issues. Distraction instead keeps faith at the margins of life. And if there is anything that Christianity cannot abide, it is marginality. Christianity is a life-claiming faith. Thus Jesus insisted in language that seems insensitive at least and harsh and narrow at worst that if we would follow him, we must leave all. We must take him as Lord. There is a peculiar blasphemy in saying to the Christ, "I have too much on my mind to crowd in thoughts of you."

When other generations appear and if their historians categorize the character of our times, they will give us a variety of names. It's possible that some of them might seem belittling and insulting compared with our opinion of ourselves. But whatever name the future may give our times, the issue of distraction will be part of it. And what we leave for any possible future generation will depend very much on how we cope, in our time, with our distractions. Especially those of us who seek to be heard in the midst of all these competing voices.

THE DISTRACTED HEART

Our world insists itself upon us daily. Everything seems to demand our undivided devotion. Our job, our spouse, our family, our pursuits—even the gym or the current diet has just such a priority for us. Each of these competes with the other every day. Who will win?

Add to this the inner noise of heart and mind, all the unsettled issues of life that keep us awake at night, that never seem to quiet down, that keep imposing themselves upon us. And then somewhere in the midst of all this comes the singular importance of God. Ah, God. Could it be that in our day God might be reduced to one distraction among many? Ouch.

It seems there is an "urgency to all things" in our market-driven culture that makes focused attention on any one thing difficult for any of us. When everything appears to have equally compelling importance, that which is worthy of exclusive devotion seems to be at the mercy of the moment and all that distracts us from it.

How do you speak into such times? As a pastor I face the issue every week: how to take captive for God the uncaptivated, distracted heart that is forever reaching for the remote.

Steve Elliott, senior pastor, First Alliance Church, Lexington, Kentucky

3

THE DISTRACTED PREACHER

Ezekiel had a tough assignment. He was a priest in Israel, but now God was calling him to be a prophet as well. Many of the ablest people in his nation—perhaps a majority—had been taken captive by the Babylonians. Now it was Ezekiel's job to minister to these people in captivity. At the least they were lonely and dispirited. They were far from home geographically and even farther away emotionally and spiritually. They had believed that God was on their side. The most celebrated fact of their heritage was the story of how centuries earlier God had delivered them from the bondage of Egypt. Now they were in bondage again, to a nation that seemed to be altogether as difficult as ancient Egypt had been.

I won't venture to assert what Ezekiel should have said to the captives, but I'm sure of where he had to say it. His message was not one to be sent from a headquarters building in Jerusalem, not even a building partly in shambles. The person speaking to the captives had to be someone who was suffering the same despair, spiritual confusion and general hopelessness as the people in his audience.

Here's how Ezekiel describes it, in the classic language of the King

James Version: "Then I came to them of the captivity at Telabib, that dwelt by the river of Chebar, and I sat where they sat, and remained there astonished among them seven days" (Ezek 3:15). "I sat where they sat." That simple phrase should be a mantra with preachers who choose to live within the same boundaries of pain and despair as their congregants and who realize that their location is a major part of their authority to speak. Only after seven days of silence did the Spirit of God tell the prophet the nature of his calling and give him a word to speak to the people.

No one has any business exegeting pain from a distance. Or prosperity and success, either, come to think of it. The best credentials are in the hands of those who are able to be "astonished" with the people they're trying to exhort or console. Of course, there's a hazard in sitting by the river of Chebar along with the captives: namely, that we may in time become so afflicted with the setting that we lose our ability to help others see beyond their conditions. It's good to sit where they sit as long as we can stand up and lead. The prophet must also maintain a prophetic distance—that is, the ability not only to diagnose the situation but to declare remedies and lead the way.

We Sit Where They Sit

As for the Age of Distraction, we preachers and teachers are susceptible to the same distractions as the people to whom we minister. We are party to the same culture patterns, we use the same gadgets, and we hear most of the same sales pitches. Indeed, in some ways we may be more susceptible than those we're trying to lead. Our work requires us to be available to people, so we seek the gadgetry that makes us available, even though the equipment brings distractions with it. If we have sensitive pastoral hearts, the ring or vibration of a cell phone is compelling. And of course there's always the pride element:

we like to think that we're with it—that we're as up to date as our most sophisticated secular counterparts.

Once again I have to say that it has always been so. That is, if we twenty-first-century spiritual leaders are prone to distractions that invade our spiritual concentration, it was the same with our vocational ancestors. G. A. Studdert-Kennedy, that most driven and dedicated of Anglican priests during World War I and the few years following in his short life, described the issue in his short poem "Temptation":

Pray! Have I prayed! When I'm worn with all my praying!
When I've bored the blessed angels with my battery of prayer!
It's the proper thing to say—but it's only saying, saying,
And I cannot get to Jesus for the glory of her hair.[1]

Or we could go farther back to the incomparable John Donne. He dared to let the people of his community know about the struggles of their esteemed cleric and he did so, strangely enough, during a funeral sermon for a member of his parish, Sir William Cokayne, in late 1620. Listen: "I throw myself down in my chamber, and I call in and invite God and his angels thither, and when they are there, I neglect God and his angels, for the noise of a fly, for the rattling of a coach, for the whining of a door."

All of this reminds us that while the times have changed in some details—the sources of the distractions and the means by which those distractions are delivered—the pastor in his or her study has always been susceptible to distraction. Paul must surely have hoped that his guard would stop humming that first-century show tune. Bunyan no doubt had to deal with insects and assorted vermin as he thought his way through *Pilgrim's Progress*. And who can guess the physical and emotional intrusions that assailed Dietrich Bonhoeffer day after day in his imprisonment!

"Well," a jaded twenty-first-century pastor might answer, "at least they didn't have to contend with a cell phone." And of course that contemporary colleague has a point, if a rather insensitive one. The pastor might be especially inclined to such self-pity if he had heard earlier that morning that there are now six billion cell phones in active use in the world, with its population of seven billion.[2] Obviously this means that many people own more than one cell phone and use however many they have, and the pastor concludes that a sizeable portion of these multiple-phone owners are trying to reach him, particularly during his study hours. Those cell phones have become the pastor's prison cell.

"As for the saints who have written from prison cells," our pastor friend continues, "well, their confinement guaranteed them a rigid schedule and hours daily without interruption." I'm sure, however, that no one is anxious to change places with the imprisoned, whether Paul, Bunyan or Bonhoeffer. Most of us will also acknowledge that it does no good to compare our circumstances with those of other generations or with particular acquaintances who seem to have advantages of concentration we don't enjoy. Such envy is not only a self-imposed distraction, it's a form of self-pity that we shouldn't entertain for long.

So let it be said, simply, that this is our generation and our time. It is here that we must minister, and it is here where we must learn to do so effectively. Let us also rejoice that we're in an ideal place to understand the people to whom we minister. Some of the problems our parishioners face in their workaday, live-a-day world are quite different from ours, and we empathize only with difficulty. But of this matter we can say with Ezekiel, "I sit where they sit." We are admirably equipped to understand their problem—and we have the opportunity to be exemplars rather than victims.

The Preacher's Soul

This is a time for the preacher to examine his or her own soul. I suggest that we do so under the insistence of the noted bioethicist Leon R. Kass. Kass is writing to our generation as a whole and not specifically to preachers, but for preachers his remarks hold special significance: "For though we are knowledgeable, powerful, and privileged with opportunities beyond our ancestors' wildest dreams, many of us remain psychically, morally, and spiritually adrift."[3]

Without a doubt you and I minister in a highly privileged time. Data is available to us literally at our fingertips. In the early days of my sermon writing I took a portable typewriter to the library to copy sentences from a book that couldn't be checked out (no photocopy machines either in that day). Now the computer can bring up the same information and vast amounts of related material that would never have occurred to me from libraries altogether out of my reach.

But with all of these riches I have a problem with my soul—and because of my calling, with the souls of the people who come under the influence of what I have to say. One isn't a social pessimist if one confesses that Kass is right when he says that many of us are psychically, morally and spiritually adrift. The evidence is all around us. Some eloquent voices are moving the ancient landmarks of moral conduct to such a degree that the boundaries are dim to the point, eventually, of nonexistence. Who shall say that the ball is out of bounds if there are no longer any side-markers? Spiritually adrift? We are now the generation not of unbelievers but of believe anything and believe quite happily and indiscriminately. Our generation is rapidly becoming the embodiment of the statement credited to G. K. Chesterton: "When men stop believing in God, they don't believe in nothing; they believe in anything."[4]

I don't mean to say that my preacher and teacher colleagues also remain, in many instances, psychically, morally and spiritually adrift, but I daresay most of us admit that this is a major hazard of our day and of our work. Statistics and anecdotal evidence make the point. We're like the doctor or nurse working in the ward of a highly infectious disease; we are in more danger than the general populace because of frequency of contact and all the more so because familiarity tends to breed carelessness.

And if we preachers and teachers become psychically, morally and spiritually adrift, we present a particular hazard, because we deal daily in issues of the human soul. If our souls are adrift, multiplied other souls are in danger. So in a world of distractions, we are under special admonishment to keep our spiritual bearings. We are compelled, under God, to be selective in what gets our attention, because what gets our attention gets us—and what gets us gets the attention of numbers of other people who pay attention to us.

Which is to say that when we give our minds and souls (and, of course, our time) to ideas, thoughts, solicitations and desires, the impact is far-reaching. Ultimately it is eternally so, but even in the passing business of the day it is significantly so.

So a heavy burden is on us. As preachers and teachers we are, like it or not, connoisseurs of ideas. We're supposed to know more about ideas and insights and to be better judges of their worth. And because we are called to represent eternity, we're supposed to know more about the proper use of time, which is our currently available symbol of eternity. Therefore, in a world of a constant "din in the head," to use Cynthia Ozick's phrase,[5] we need to know what themes matter most and be the most selective in what we "listen" to. It is from our souls that the souls of others are fed and influenced. This is a hard, almost impossible assignment, but it comes with our calling.

The challenge is clear. We preachers and teachers must become discriminating in our taste. There is more "stuff" out there than we can even sample, let alone give our extended attention. In the Lorelei legend of the maiden who threw herself into the Rhine River because of a faithless lover and ever after enchanted sailors to death by her song, there was only one hazardous port. But for our time, the mental, moral and spiritual Lorelei have a thousand different voices and melodic combinations, with faces and costumes to appeal not only to particular people but to the same people at particular times.

I think you know without my saying so that our situation is fearfully complex. On one hand we need to know the world in which our people live. But it is no longer the world of our great-grandparents, where nearly all the people in the pews had the same occupation—say, dairy farming or working at the local factory—and essentially the same education. Now the preacher looks out on vocations that did not exist a decade ago, let alone a century ago. Theoretically, the congregation is more educated than the one our predecessors knew because there are more college graduates. But it's likely they're more specialized, not more educated. They very well may know less literature, history and basic civics than some of the eighth grade graduates of a century ago.

But to preach to a collection of specialists means the preacher has to have some understanding of the particular knowledge and interests with which these people live. When I was a pastor I hoped that I might in some measure be a Renaissance person, knowing enough about a variety of interests that I could anticipate what interested my people. Perhaps the best we can hope for now is to know at least enough to ask intelligent questions and to listen with an attentive mind. But we can't know it all and of course we shouldn't pretend to. And since we can't know everything, we must be highly discriminating in the knowledge we pursue.

Just over a century ago Charles Edward Jefferson preached a

sermon on the narrowness of Jesus. I assume Jefferson was playing on the prejudices of his time and of his New York City congregation in that it was a period that gloried in being broad minded. But what he said was true then and is more appropriate than ever to the time in which we now live and think and work. Jefferson insisted that there were "a thousand good things" that a good person in first-century Palestine might do, but that Jesus left 999 of them untouched and "confined himself to the one thing which he believed his Heavenly Father had given him to do."[6] I think of the language of Luke's Gospel. When Jesus discerned that the time of his ordained purpose was near, "he set his face to go to Jerusalem" (Lk 9:51 NRSV). This meant he was rejected by a village in Samaria where he apparently wanted to minister, and in a series of instances he rejected potential disciples because they had some temporary impediment (Lk 9:52-62). Jesus had one goal in mind. He knew the price involved, but the issue was so clear that he had tunnel vision: all he could see was Jerusalem and the purpose of God that lay before him there.

Our assignment is difficult and complicated. In order to be perceptive about the times in which we live, we have to know as much as possible about as many things as possible. Yet we also have to focus singularly on our eternal commitment. This is difficult but not out of reach. In the cacophony of competing sounds we ask a constant question: What does this have to do with the human souls I'm trying to reach? I know that all of these competing voices come from the world of human souls, but out of it all, what is most directly at issue? This question will help us push aside the transient and the trivial. And I don't need to tell you that the transient and trivial crowd our days.

The Preacher as Pastor

This brings us to the specific issue of time. If preachers were more like newspaper columnists or some Internet bloggers, they could give all their time to research and writing. But a pastor is also counselor and administrator. I learned (though slowly!) to spend less time on minor matters of oversight and administration. I also learned that I didn't have to be an expert in everything and that there was great satisfaction in letting people know more than I did. The micromanager almost always gets lost in the micro while important matters—usually the human matters—slip by.

And, of course, if the preacher is a compassionate pastor—as should be the case—time management is a major issue. Shall a pastor see people only by appointment and accept telephone calls only at certain hours of the day? Personally, I never felt I had that privilege. Obviously I didn't take telephone calls when I was already in personal conference with someone, but otherwise the calls came through. Nor did I employ a filter system via the receptionist or secretary ("May I ask the purpose of your call?"). I learned that such an answer would likely turn away the neediest person, the timid one who had finally worked up the courage to seek help.

So I allowed my potential study time and the time spent on organizational details to be interrupted, which happened often and sometimes at length. If I were to live my life over, I would live by the same rule. Mind you, I'm more than sympathetic to the pastor who is visited several times a week by kindly folks who have nothing else to do and want the pastor to fill their time for them. I've lived there. And I know that there are some people who want an appointment every week because the pastor is the only listening ear they can afford. I've lived there too. I suspect some who read this will decide that I am the kind of pastor who allowed his life to be controlled by other people. Perhaps. But I'd rather my life were controlled by the needs, or even the perceived needs, of people than by many other possible controlling forces.

I mention the issue of people-interruptions, however, to talk about a partial solution. I learned as the years went by that my greatest loss of time when interrupted by the telephone or the physical visitor was not the interruption itself but the time necessary for re-entry. With the telephone call completed it's easy to go after coffee, iced tea or a Dr Pepper, to chat for a few minutes with a fellow worker, or to rearrange some books that caught our attention during the telephone visit. The simple, solid secret is to go back to work without delay. When an interruption comes you may do well to break in the middle of a sentence rather than saying, "Wait until I finish this paragraph," because it's easier to re-enter in the middle of a sentence than in the middle of a vacuum of thought.

FIRST THINGS FIRST

Dr. Kalas has identified one of the greatest obstacles that I face in sermon preparation as well as devotional living—distraction. The most effective mechanism I have discovered for overcoming distraction is practicing "First things first." I confess that I do not accomplish this every day. However, on those days that I do, I spend significant time in spiritual formation and sermon preparation during the morning hours. Being a morning person, I seem to have more capacity to withstand the temptation of distraction in the early hours. That is when my thought process is clearest, my energy level highest and my focus greatest.

Debbie Wallace-Padgett, Bishop of the United Methodist Church, North Alabama Conference

The Internet and Distraction

Obviously, however, the greatest source of interruptive distraction in our time is not the telephone or the friendly drop-in but the various forms of the Internet. The only way to win this battle is to establish early in the day the time or two in the morning or afternoon when we will check for messages. Quite simply, the secret is for us to control the Internet and not let the Internet control us. The Internet has no feelings to be hurt if you ignore it for two hours. Nor does the Internet have a sense of courtesy that keeps it from interrupting you. It is our servant, and if we allow it to be our master, we deserve our sentence of slavery.

In its own way the Internet can be a blessing in the world of distractions because it compels us to make choices. It is the ultimate democratization of ideas. I remember the long-ago world of Columbus Circle in New York City, when religious speakers, political and economic radicals, and others who wanted an audience for reasons known only to themselves could get hearers for as long as someone would listen. Some, of course, kept speaking even when the audience had moved on to the next voice. Who could have imagined that a day would come when untold thousands would speak their mind to equally untold millions—and without the price of being shouted down by hecklers? This is what the Internet has become: a worldwide Columbus Circle, or a London Hyde Park, where anyone can express an opinion and no one needs to show credentials or pass through a filter designed to eliminate those less qualified to speak.

The Internet will take as much of our time as we allow it to have. And it will invade our hours so subtly that we won't know where the time has gone, let alone realize what value we might have found in a different venue elsewhere. Without a doubt the Internet offers great wealth. But we will pan away acres of sand for a few grains of gold unless we have the intellectual stamina to discriminate between what is worthy and what is not. Contemporary scholar Leon Botstein warns that "the wealth of possibilities opened up by the Internet can easily lead the writer astray. . . . We need new talents, new skills and a sophisticated ability to sort genuine connections from spurious ones."[7]

Those of us who love information are especially susceptible to the Internet and to other forms of communication. This is good. But it is counterproductive in the extreme unless we establish standards of exclusion. Some experts refer to this as the culling process, the elimination of those things that don't matter or that matter only marginally. Cull by category, they say, and thus eliminate great sections without spending time in decisions. For years I thought I couldn't discard a periodical until I'd read everything in it. I've since learned that there are many subjects of which I need to know little or nothing, so I skip over many sections of the newspaper and print periodicals and skim the top of the Internet.

Here's a major factor in the culling process: a preacher's own personality. Most communicators have a vast variety of interests; this is part of what makes them interesting to listen to. Weigh your instinctive interests alongside the needs of the people to whom you minister until you can see where you can best invest your particular skills for the particular needs you serve.

Counsel from Another Time

Perhaps it seems counterintuitive to go back a century for counsel. On the other hand, perhaps we need to step out of the present malaise in order to clear our minds. George Herbert Morrison was one of Scotland's finest preachers from the late nineteenth century through the first quarter of the twentieth, in an era when the Scottish pulpit was at its best. Part of his secret was that he believed in the value of good preaching. The flyleaf on a recent collection of his sermons notes, "Intently focused on his call to preach the Word, he refused many offers to serve on committees and in leadership positions that might have distracted [that word again!] him from his preaching and writing."[8]

These are particular distractions for the preacher and teacher. They relate to career, to loyalty to one's denominational body, to places of responsibility within the civic community. These are distractions with which generations of spiritual leaders have had to cope, and the claim of such distractions is both legitimate and enticing. One wants to be part of larger endeavors, to exercise influence in civic and ecclesiastical bodies, and such leaders are needed. So how do we divide our time and energy and indeed our spiritual passion?

When a young preacher asked Dr. Morrison the secret of his fine preaching skills, Morrison answered, "I can think of nothing, except that young preachers will do well to guard against the tendency to rush which is the bane of modern life. The habit of unprofitable bustle and rush, the present-day preoccupation with small affairs and engagements, is withholding many good things from us. For myself it is essential that I have leisure to brood and meditate."[9] The language sounds quaint; perhaps that's not surprising since it comes from nearly a century ago. And we're inclined to smile condescendingly when Dr. Morrison speaks of "the tendency to rush which is the bane of modern life." To us his world seems almost medieval.

But after we've smiled we need to listen. If Dr. Morrison was afraid of being preoccupied "with small affairs and engagements," the threat to us is far greater. I suspect, however, that it is precisely the "small affairs" that have multiplied, not major ones, and no doubt the voices of those "small affairs" have become more shrill and incessant. But they have become no more significant. We need the "leisure," if we may call it that, "to brood and meditate." We need it all the more because the number of other voices has increased and the other voices are increasingly attractive and distracting.

So the preacher must learn to wait, to ponder, to wrestle with Jacob's angel. The preacher and teacher must come to believe ever more deeply in the value of what they do. We must hold the value of our work and our message alongside the transient claims that pursue us so that we can properly determine how to spend our time. Charles Jefferson, also speaking a century ago, insisted that he prepared his sermons by preparing himself: "Self preparation is the most difficult work a preacher has to do."[10] And that begins with eliminating matters that are secondary at best and inconsequential at worst.

TOOLS FOR HANDLING DISTRACTION

Distractions come in a variety of shapes, sizes and colors with a multitude of sounds and smells. Distractions are a part of our personal as well as our professional lives. We simply have to accept that they have always been and will always be part of our lives. (As I attempt to write this paragraph the misaligned sprinkler in the front of our house hits the window to my office as music plays on the TV in our living room while my wife and daughters chase after the family dog who has stolen an artifact from my daughter's bedroom.)

There are three tools I use to help handle the distractions I experience in my day. First, I have a "Do not disturb" sign that I hang on the door to my office when I absolutely must work on a project. My secretary knows and respects the fact that when this sign is out she is to take messages when calls come in and to only interrupt me with drop-in visitors if it is an emergency.

Next, I know how to not answer my phone. Letting a call go to voicemail is an important lesson I learned early in my ministry. Voicemails can be retrieved and messages processed as time allows.

Third, I keep a stack of blank three-by-five index cards and a Sharpie pen close at hand on my desk with a wire file basket as my inbox. If I choose a distraction to break into my day, I simply write down what I was working on an index card and place it in my in-basket. That way I can come back to it as soon as I'm finished with the distraction.

Scott Andrews, pastor, Shepherd of the Valley United Methodist Church, Indio, California

4

THE DISTRACTED CONGREGATION

If we preachers have a problem with distraction, the problem is multiplied several times for the people to whom we speak. The motto on the wall of the preacher's study may be, "Be still and know that I am God," but the unwritten message for many of our congregants is something like, "Hurry up. You're already late."

For us preachers the hero is (or ought to be) the saint—those people so apt at making choices that they cut through the paraphernalia of life and center on what matters most. Saints have learned how to keep their souls fixed on true north; that is, they have learned how to move toward God with all their heart, soul, mind and strength. The people in the pews have heroes, too, and their heroes tend to be achievers. Whether the hero is an athlete, a political personality, a homemaker or an executive, you can expect him or her to be a winner. And while the people in the pews may believe that part of their achievement is a result of their character (with prayer perhaps factored in), they're likely to see God more as an aid than as the goal. It isn't easy to be a preacher, but it isn't easy to be a layperson either.

Many of the preacher's distractions are in our work and thus not far removed from issues of God and godly living. The people in the congregation also live in a world of work and God is not usually its center, but they bring that world to church with them. I remember a barber in the church of my teenage years. "You know why I sit near the front of the church?" he asked one day. Without waiting for my answer he continued, "Cutting hair is an art with me, and I can't keep my mind on the sermon when I see bad haircuts in front of me. So I just sit up close." He recognized his primary distraction and found a solution.

When I was a pastor in Green Bay, Wisconsin, a number of Green Bay Packers football players and coaches became part of our congregation. A defensive lineman (who was elected posthumously into the National Football League Hall of Fame) had attended church faithfully from January into June, but as summer training camp drew near he told me he would find it hard to come to church from then until the football season was over. "I've been playing football since I was in the eighth grade, and I know every time I get positioned for a play that one bad twist of a knee could end my career," he told me. "It's hard, preacher, to sit in church on a Sunday when I'm going out to the stadium in just a few hours."

Such are the people who come to church: teachers and students, homemakers and beauticians, executives and truck drivers, laboratory assistants and bank tellers, farmers and retired people. Their work occupies a large percentage of their waking hours—some remember what that work used to be, and some worry about what they'll do if they lose their job or their business goes bankrupt. Jesus drew his parables from shepherds, farmers and homemakers, using the distraction of work as a means of soul entry. It's a wise entryway to the soul for us, too, but the doors have multiplied in such specific and particular ways that it would be hard in most congregations to use vocational "for instances" that apply to more than a few.

Two Groups of People

Broadly speaking, the preacher tries to relate to two audiences. There's that body of people who are already committed to Christ to one degree or another, and then there are those who are marginal or as yet unreached. We see the first group more often because they participate more regularly in worship and may also be in some study group or position of leadership. We shouldn't assume, however, that all of them are fully committed to Christ. In truth, some of them are in church or in study or fellowship gatherings more out of habit than by the passion of convinced discipleship. For such individuals, church is what they do; the language is familiar to them and they don't necessarily ask themselves why they "belong" or to what degree they belong. But whatever their inner state, the people in this first group are the ones we count on—numerically, financially and spiritually.

The second group is made up of people who participate occasionally if at all. If a pollster were to ask these people about their church affiliation, they might name your church. In some cases this would surprise you. But if we have a heart for those outside the kingdom, this second group includes not only the people who appear occasionally on the radar of our church life but also numbers of people we've probably never met. They belong to that indeterminate group we refer to as "the people we'd like to reach." It would be hard for us to draw a profile of these folks—and perhaps it's just as well that we don't, because in making such a profile we might eliminate a great many people who are closer to us than we realize.

We dare not neglect either of these groups. We shouldn't see them as competitors for our time or our attention, and we shouldn't pit them against each other in our programming and pastoral care. Of course it's easy to give all our attention to the people currently with us, and pragmatism says we'd better because this is where our support comes from. On the other hand, a passion for evangelism may convince us that the sheep in the fold can take care of themselves while we concentrate on the lost. A sheep is a sheep, and one is not to be prized above the other. The shepherd may leave those in the fold while seeking the lost, but the wise shepherd makes sure the ninety-nine are safely enclosed so that they don't become the newly lost while we're pursuing those we know to be lost.

These two groups are both distracted. Those in the first group probably hear better when the preacher speaks because they have a relationship with him or her (though this depends greatly on the preacher's willingness to spend time with the congregation beyond the worship hour), but both groups live in the culture of a thousand insistent voices. Thus sometimes it's as much of a challenge to hold onto those in the first group and strengthen their faith as it is to get the attention of those outside.

I recall a sentence we used to hear in the grade school classes of my boyhood. The teacher spoke it emphatically: "I want your undivided attention!" I wonder if today's grade school teachers ever employ that sentence. Is there such a thing in our clamorous world as "undivided attention," or does the teacher or preacher have to settle for a place not only among other attentions, but among appeals that are likely to be more naturally attractive? Come to think of it, the classroom teacher has a certain edge on the preacher in the pass/fail power at the semester's end. The preacher preaches with eternity in view, but eternity seems farther away than the end of the fall or spring term.

Where Success Is Spelled Excess

So who are these people to whom we preach? For one thing, they are people who subscribe naturally and deeply to the doctrine of abundance. They have no clear line between what is necessary and what is desired. The natural competitiveness of the human soul ("If my neighbor has it, I should have it too") is stimulated hundreds of times daily by advertising that says the same thing, thus producing humans who want not only enough but more than enough. The late Peter Gomes, longtime dean of the Harvard Chapel, said that of the generation of preachers he had been observing, few "were prepared to take on the perceptions and deceptions of a culture that defined success in terms of excess."[1]

It's difficult for us to keep our bearings in a time when excess is considered not only normal but commendable. And as surely as two cars are not enough and television screens are never large enough, even success itself is never big enough. The vague vision of some success not yet achieved dulls the joy of the success recently achieved. Have we won the Super Bowl? Then next year we must accomplish greater success by being a repeater. Has our quaint little restaurant, the dream we cherished for so long, become a place our town or neighborhood talks about? Then perhaps we can morph it into a chain. Success has an insatiable appetite.

I'm not talking about economics; I'm talking about living. I'm saying that we shouldn't measure living simply by length and breadth but remember the greater importance of depth. Our culture insists that we broaden ourselves, and of course this idea has merit. But we ought also to deepen ourselves. We don't necessarily need more of anything except the ability to appreciate what we already have. The richest people are not those who have the most but those who enjoy and use wisely what they have. Unfortunately, we're preaching to many people who consider such an idea rather strange. It's all right, they reason, for a Mother Teresa type, but it's probably not "normal." Not in their world, at any rate.

Perhaps so. But it might prove to be healthy, satisfying and more real than they can imagine. If we preachers take Jesus seriously, we're calling people to that kind of life—and in doing so we're calling them to a kind of life that cuts across the grain of what they hear during most of their waking hours.

The fact is, this living for excess hasn't proved fulfilling. Yes, some things are basic enough that they are truly important to happy living. Surveys show that people in wealthier nations are happier than those in poorer ones. Obviously we'd rather have enough to eat, proper heating and, yes, even air conditioning once we experience its benefits. But professor Barry Schwartz reports that at a certain point after a nation moves from poverty to "adequate subsistence," additional wealth has little if any effect on happiness. "You find as many happy people in Poland as in Japan, for example, even though the average Japanese is almost ten times richer than the average Pole," he writes.[2]

Surveys also show that if you compare happiness in a given nation over different time periods, it is still clear that excess doesn't make for happiness. Adjusted for inflation, the per capita income of Americans has more than doubled during the past forty years. This means that the percentage of homes with dishwashers has increased from nine percent to fifty percent, the percentage with clothes dryers has grown from twenty percent to seventy percent, and homes with air conditioning have increased from 15 percent to 73 percent. But with all of that, there has been no gain in the level of happiness.[3] We've gotten more stuff, and although it is stuff we think makes life richer and more enjoyable, our happiness has not increased with the stuff.

These are the people to whom we preach. They hear us say, "Seek ye first the kingdom of God and his righteousness," but they hear other preachers—the shopping mall and the ever-present voices of advertising—say that if they get certain pleasures, privileges and time freedom, they will be happier than they were without those things. This hasn't proved to be true, however, and one wonders how long it will be before the distraction of "more" is recognized as a fraud. Perhaps never, because one of the elements in the "more" argument is that if you're not satisfied with what you've gotten, it's because you still haven't gotten enough—there's lots more out there to try. So something tells you that maybe the next "more" will be the one that fits your psyche.

I think of Jesus' parable of the rich landowner—the man whose harvest was so bountiful that he said, "Here's what I'll do. I'll tear down my barns and build bigger ones." And then, "Take it easy! Eat, drink, and enjoy yourself." God told the man that he was a fool, because that night he would die (Lk 12:18-20). I'm sure the text is referring to eternal death and that the night was the one in which this man would meet his Maker. But we are also true to the text if we realize that this kind of living, this constant striving for more, is a process of slow death. All the beauty of life is slowly consumed in the search for still more. Little time if any is spent in rejoicing in what is, because attention is focused on what still might be. Such souls are experiencing a lingering death and an increasingly tragic one since their lives have fewer and fewer fulfillments.

Jesus' parable reminds us that the fascination with "more" is not a twenty-first-century phenomenon. It's interesting, isn't it, that it was just as real and as deadly in the first-century agricultural economy as in today's corporate, sports and entertainment world. The difference, however, is that fewer people in the first-century world had reason for grandiose dreams, and there were few if any voices that said, "You, too, can aspire to the world of expanding barns." The possibility of more is now far more widespread, and even those with the least reason to hope are exposed to voices that encourage unlikely expectations. We shouldn't be surprised if in this pursuit people turn to crime or drugs or shady investment schemes or the daily lottery. This is the culture to which we preach, sometimes including the faithful people who come to our women's Bible study, our men's prayer breakfasts or our weekend youth retreat (they're never too young to be so enculturated, and few are too old).

As for the young, they seem always to have been restless. We expressed it differently in our time and place, but restlessness is part of the growing-up process. Our culture doesn't help. Some of the most earnest parents are on a constant run ("We're the family chauffeurs," a father and mother told me, with a laugh of resignation) to take their children to the variety of sports events and enrichment opportunities, but unfortunately they spend little time in conversation, sharing or listening. Activity has crowded out relationship. Particularly, activity has crowded out eating together as a family, saying grace together and having time to talk about the small stuff of the day. And small stuff is wonderful, because it's the basic setting in which life is unfolding—and thus the setting where faith is paramount.

I admire the suburban mother who told her children that there would be no more than one sport per semester. "I was told I was being cruel," she said, "but now I hear, 'It's sort of fun not to be running all the time.'" It is not an easy time to be a parent, especially in the single-parent home or the home where both parents are employed—and in all homes, because the culture around us keeps asking for more. The world around us seeks to shape us into its form, and families need great insight, patience and courage to dare an ultimate course.

Quantity and Quality

Several years ago families began using the term "quality time." The word and the idea had merit. Unfortunately, the idea was misused in that it became a way of excusing oneself from the unforgivable issue of quantity. Try as we will to organize our social relationships into quality patterns, much of the best of quality comes simply in the context of quantity. That is, we have to be together often enough and for long enough periods that quality comes to birth. In our hurried lives we may not realize that there isn't time enough to have hours left over for quality after ordinariness and mediocrity have made their claims.

Eugene Peterson, who is known to most people for his vigorous rendition of the Scriptures in contemporary English, continues to think and write as a pastor. For more than three decades he served a Presbyterian church in Maryland of which he was the founding pastor. "What I wasn't prepared for," he writes, "was the low level of interest that the men and women in my congregation had in God and the scriptures, prayer and their souls. Not that they didn't believe and value these things; they just weren't very interested." He had been schooled, Peterson continues, "in the company of Moses and David; my congregation kept emotional and mental company with television celebrities and star athletes. I was reading Karl Barth and John Calvin; they were reading Ann Landers and *People* magazine."[4]

Peterson is recalling the world of forty and fifty years ago. The issue is dramatically intensified in this second decade of the twenty-first century. Yet even before the dominating influence of the computer and its still more omnipresent offspring, the competition for time and attention was being taken over by secular voices. We can hardly imagine the frontier homes of the mid-nineteenth century, where the only reading material was likely to be the Bible and the weekly denominational paper. And it is even more difficult to imagine seventeenth-century America as Larry Whitham describes it: "Published sermons outnumbered almanacs, newspapers, and political pamphlets by four to one. New England was the most literate society in the world."[5] This literacy was built on the Puritan conviction that the population should be taught to read so that they might read the Scriptures. Their descendants would be surprised to know this. Perhaps, unfortunately, they might also be amused.

There is little value, however, in mourning what has happened. When it looks as if your team is about to score a touchdown only to be intercepted near the goal line and the ball carried down the field seventy or eighty yards, the defensive unit can't waste time sorrowing over the change in fortune. Rather, they must learn quickly how they are to stay in the game when they no longer control the ball.

I remember sermons from my childhood warning that we were in a time when people "will not endure sound doctrine; but after their own lusts shall they heap to themselves teachers, having itching ears" (2 Tim 4:3 KJV). Obviously this warning is not limited to a particular time, since the apostle was writing it in the first century. But the warnings I heard in my boyhood were pre-television, to say nothing of pre-Internet. The pastors and evangelists were warning us primarily about religious teachers that might promulgate false doctrine. In this twenty-first century our most engaging, persuasive and ever-present teachers are not in the pulpit or the classroom but in our homes, our public eating places and even in our automobiles. And it seems that the more they tell us, the more our ears itch.

Our itching may not be of the highest order. Not, at least, in its demonstrated form or in the ways we seek to satisfy it. And as far as my personal tastes are concerned, I don't think it is only the church and its ministry that is suffering. I think the wider world of secular publishing and entertainment is also dealing with a serious decline in taste and judgment.

Nevertheless I see another factor contributing to our "itching ears."

I ponder Saint Augustine: "You have made us for yourself, and our heart is restless until it rests in you."[6] However poor or jaded its taste, the ear that itches is expressing the longing of a restless heart. It may be absorbed in distractions and it may seek still more distractions. But somewhere, inevitably, as sure as there is God, the hunger is for God.

Preachers and teachers must remember this as they prepare to speak to their congregants. Perhaps they should confess that in many ways their gathering is not so much a congregation as an audience. Its members are not to be condemned for their spiritual illiteracy or maligned for what can seem to be intellectual poor taste. They are people on a search, whether they know it or not, a search as old as Eden and as sure as eternity. Are they sometimes making notes regarding next week's appointments rather than notes on the sermon? Is the throbbing in their breast pocket a cell phone rather than the heartbeat of holy longing? Are they thinking more about this afternoon's football game than about what we're saying?

If so, you and I can be rightly troubled and challenged but should not despair. In the midst of all the voices there is still the most persistent one: "Adam, Eve, where are you?" The preacher and teacher must remember that no matter how many ideas and desires are laying claim on the person in the pew, the voice of the Holy Spirit still calls. And the degree to which that call is heard depends in significant measure on the preacher and teacher: on our ability on the one hand to sense the hungers of our people and to understand the clamor of voices that engage them and on the other hand to hear the voice of God's Spirit in our own hearts and message.

We need to remember that the longing for God is older than the longing for more and that the sensation the secular world sells cannot be fully satisfied short of God. This is true whether the people to whom we preach seem to be an audience or a true congregation of the people of God. All are equally valuable in God's sight, equally cherished and pursued. And all of them have an equal need and longing for God, no matter how covered over it may be with today's stuff and tomorrow's fears and desires.

DISTRACTED WITH GOD

"Distracted" is an interesting choice of terms to describe our culture. I say that it is interesting because this word normally carries the connotation of failing to focus on something upon which one had implicitly or explicitly agreed to focus. For example, when two people are engaging in an intimate conversation there is an unspoken agreement between them that they will give the other their undivided attention. If one of them fails to meet this obligation of politeness he will apologize by explaining that he was distracted.

The problem with preaching in our contemporary culture is that no consensus exists about the appropriate subject of our focus. Historically, the practice of preaching has depended heavily on the assumption that God deserves our attention. Such an assumption can no longer be safely held. Thus, our culture is more disoriented than it is distracted.

In the face of such a culture, perhaps the greatest temptation of preaching is to recognize such disorientation and to alter accordingly. The prevailing wisdom calls this relevance; I call it surrender. The problem with this approach is that preaching becomes just as disoriented as culture, because it agrees that there is no central focus around which our lives ought to rightfully revolve. In such an understanding, man no longer exists to glorify God. Rather, we are not sure why man exists, but we do know that we like to be entertained, and we find it useful to do what we can to make each other kinder and more highly functional while we are here. Thus preaching devolves into an endless attempt to keep up with what people want to hear, what is amusing to them, and what topic is of immediate interest. That is, preaching becomes just one more distraction competing with many others.

In response to such a situation the faithful preacher must refuse to agree to the tacit assumption of modernity that the other concerns of life are more important than God. The pastor must be deeply formed in the classic disciplines of the Christian faith so that his life will not be disoriented. He must be correctly oriented if he would serve as a guide to a lost culture. The pastor must be "distracted" with God.

Drew Martin, pastor, First United Methodist Church, Clover, South Carolina

5

THE BENEFITS OF DISTRACTION

Meryl Streep is known not only as an award-winning actress but also for a nearly uncanny ability to "become" the character she portrays. When an interviewer asked Ms. Streep what she "loved to do," she answered that she liked everything. "There's just not anything I don't like to do. That's the problem. It means I'm very distractible."[1]

There seems to be a disconnect here. Those who have studied Ms. Streep's work marvel at the intensity with which she immerses herself in a character, studying the person—especially when it is a historical personality—until that person is completely real to her. How can a person capable of such concentration see herself as "very distractible"?

But then an opposing question comes to mind. How could the actress portray such a variety of personalities unless she was inclined to distraction? If she were interested only in politics, or sports, or art, she would be effective only when portraying such a person. Worse, she would never find out if there was more to her than her present area of interest. In a sense, in fact, she would spend her career portraying Meryl Streep—and without giving herself an opportunity to know who Meryl Streep is, because certainly there is more to Ms.

Streep than would appear on earlier exposures. Instead, she has reached into all kinds of worlds because she is "distractible." This reminds us that some of the most creative minds are also the most distractible. And often, also, among the most interesting.

The Benefits of Distraction

The business of this chapter, to put it directly, is to recognize that distractions themselves are not necessarily bad. Indeed, distractions can be very good, even essential to our growth as individuals and as a human race. Nevertheless, by their nature distractions often prevent our concentrating on tasks that simply must be done and done well— that is, with concentration. Almost surely distractions are more often counterproductive than productive. Thus the issue is this: How can we winnow and sift our distractions so that we invest our time in matters that are good and productive yet not eliminate those distractions that stimulate creativity? How can we train our spiritual and intellectual tastes so that we deal wisely with our distractions—especially since most distractions come in such form and with such speed that we rarely have time for a full-scale analysis. We need to become nearly instinctual in dealing with the intrusions that are part of every hour of our days.

Let's pause for a moment to realize that only in recent generations have we come to honor specialists—that is, individuals who concentrate so intently on some area of knowledge or skill that they are almost oblivious to other areas of life and interest. In previous generations the extent of knowledge in any given field was limited enough that the mind of a genius couldn't find enough room for exploration in any single field. As a result, the great minds—the kind we would classify as "genius"—weren't easily pigeonholed. Blaise Pascal was a mathematician, a philosopher, a scientist and an essayist—and with it all, a Christian of such passionate faith that it could well have been said that God was all of his life. Frances Willard was an educator, an orator, a master administrator and organizer, and a political leader (though she never had the right to vote). When historians name America's two or three greatest presidents, Abraham Lincoln is inevitably on the list as a great leader and reformer. But if he had not gone into politics, he could well have been remembered as one of America's greatest writers. I know of few essayists or poets who put words together with greater beauty. And though some in Lincoln's own generation considered him an irreligious man and some today still find it difficult to delineate Lincoln's theology, others refer to him as America's greatest lay theologian. It is difficult to discuss the will of God or the activity of God in human history without quoting him. When someone mentions the name Michelangelo, we think first of the artist who painted the ceiling of the Sistine Chapel, but then we recall that he was equally famous as the sculptor who gave us the Pietà. But he was also an architect and, not so incidentally, a poet. Were Pascal, Willard, Lincoln and Michelangelo simply very distractible? If so, let us give thanks to God!

Or for another look at specialization, consider the world of sports. A generation or two ago, the premier college athletes were those who won letters in the three "major" sports: baseball, football and basketball. Today the high school athlete who stars in both basketball and football is told by the university that courts him that he will have to choose one or the other. Fifty years ago football fans paid special honor to the "triple threat man"—someone who could pass, run the ball and kick. Today football is a world of specialists. Both the punter and the kicker kick a football, but it's hard to imagine a professional team that would try to combine the two. Indeed, they may even have two kickers, one for the long distance work of the kickoff and the other for the accuracy of the field goal and the point after touchdown. The punter and the kicker know they must spend their hours perfecting their specialty and not allow themselves to be distracted by thoughts of what it might be like to be a wide receiver.

We need specialists, no doubt about it. If someone has a rare disease, he looks for an equally rare specialist. The world of finance is so complicated that we need not only a specialist in investment but individuals who devote all their time to just one field: utilities, transportation, energy resources, pharmaceuticals—and sometimes just a subspecialty within that field.

But something in us wants to be more than specialists. Indeed, a complete specialist can easily also be a complete bore. All of us know that we live in a very big, very complex and very wonderful world. Oughtn't we to know as much about this wonderful world as possible? At the same time, however, we remind ourselves that the specialist may also be a generalist within a specialty and that the specialist deals with distraction in a different way from the rest of us.

All of which is to say there's a place for distraction. Perhaps we could even say that to be distracted is to be well-rounded. It might rightly be said, "Show me an easily distracted person and I'll show you an interesting one." Or yet again, "Show me a distractible person and I'll show you someone who is a good listener—at least for a while!"

So distraction is not all bad. In fact, it is absolutely necessary. Distraction is our learning edge. If I am interested only in what I already know, I'll never get very far beyond the boundaries of my native, undeveloped interest. Also, the edge of our field of interest often borders on a field that by its very proximity will reveal new aspects of our native territory. I'll understand my own territory better if I cross over that boundary. If I limit myself to my square acre, I'll become tiresome to myself and to others, and I'll certainly become a tedious preacher or teacher. The God whose creation includes unnumbered varieties of beetles and who continues to spill out more planets is surely a God who intends for the premier product of creation, the human being, to be a curious, exploring, growing creature. That is, a person susceptible to distraction.

In its place, this is true also in our prayer life. The thought that seems at first to intrude on our concentrating on God may be the very matter we should be discussing with God and opening up to God for insight and redemption.

Distraction as a Quality Stimulant

Perhaps we should make a case for planned distractions. That is, we might be wise to put ourselves in the path of distraction or organize some distractions into our journey. Jon Sweeney, an author and lecturer, asked himself at a recent point in his career why he was so mentally, spiritually and physically exhausted. He remembered days as a fourteen-year-old when he was working long hours at a physically exhausting job yet rarely felt tired. Sweeney explains that his earlier ability to be refreshed wasn't simply because he was young. "I was less tired then because I was more easily distracted," he says. "Today I'm good at focusing. But too much focus leads to too much stress, as well as exhaustion."[2]

There is restorative value in certain kinds of distraction. Sweeney has chosen to think fresh thoughts, to take a break for a walk or to pray for a friend or simply to look at a songbird outside his office window. Time wasted? The farthest thing from it. I submit that this in its own way is a variation on the oft-praised "power nap." The executive says that a ten-minute nap taken in a desk chair or perhaps a taxi en route to the airport gives a surge of energy out of all proportion to the time invested. A purposeful distraction can set the mind on a whole new course of creative, productive thinking.

When it comes to thinking, the straight line may not be the best path between two points. Sometimes we can even say a good word for the rabbit trail. In the race for ideas the erratic hare may do as well as the persistent tortoise if only the hare is wise enough to know when to stop, refresh itself and hit the trail again. Indeed, if the mind is bogging down to a point where everything that comes to the surface seems dull and meaningless, the thought that distracts can seem a celestial gift. If what we're thinking about is too small, the mind's restlessness is justified and we are enemies to our own productivity and growth when we try to shut it in. Sometimes what we think of as the distracted mind may more accurately be the pet dog that keeps whining and jumping for attention; the distraction may be more important than the dead end of a thought that has run its course, or that at the least is temporarily derailed.

Directing Our Distractions

G. K. Chesterton was one of those individuals with an encyclopedic mind and talent. He observed (probably from examining his own mind) that one's soul is as full of voices as a forest with the ten thousand tongues of the trees—but Chesterton warned that "some of those voices have authority and others not."[3] How do we know which distractions are worthy and which are not? How can we tell the difference so that we use our distractions without being controlled by them? There's the rub! And especially when distractions crowd upon us from every side, how in such a culture can we be distracted enough to grow yet not so distracted that we grow aimlessly and to no end? How can we get the good from distractions without their becoming ends in themselves? That is, how do we make distractions our servant and not our master?

To put it abruptly, the voice of God is a distraction to the sinner as surely as temptation to evil is a distraction to the saint. I don't do much shopping, but when I do, I use my "reward card." From time to time therefore the cash register presents me with a slip promising a discount on my favorite soft drink or candy, because by now the computer knows my appetites. The brain (sometimes in cooperation with our glands) is the ultimate computer. It knows our appetites, whether good, ill or a complex combination of both.

I've trained my mind and soul in many areas, and no doubt you have, too. I go past most of the radio stations in my automobile, most television programs and most of the pop-up ads on my computer because they have no welcome spot in my desires and interests. But other data gets my attention. Some of it is welcome and some is not. Which is to say that over a long lifetime, a remarkable conglomerate of data has taken residence in some corner or square of my brain, and it's astonishing and sometimes embarrassing to realize it's there. Some of the unworthy data that finds lodging surprises me because I can't remember ever having provided hospitality to its kind. But of course herein is the marvel of this ultimate computer, the human brain: it seems that the stuff that runs past it takes up transient residence even when I don't consciously welcome it. The apostle Paul cried "O wretched man" because of the body of death that clung to him. I sometimes want to cry, "O wretched mind! Where and when did you pick up this stuff and junk? And who shall deliver me?"

Well, there's no doubt but that God's Spirit is willing to deliver us. But it's also true that since our minds are being bombarded and solicited and seduced hundreds and even thousands of times daily, it's a constant battle. And if we are going to cooperate with God in winning this battle, we will have to be intentional in seeking to build a mentality and a psyche that is spiritually and intellectually discriminating.

I have purposely used both of the above adverbs—*spiritually* and *intellectually*. Obviously Christian preachers and teachers are concerned about the spiritual material that comes into their lives and thinking. To refer again to the apostle Paul, we know well enough that we ought to think on that which is true, holy, just, pure, lovely and worthy of praise. We know well enough that the more we feed our spirits on such quality, the more surely we will draw in more such quality. No wonder then that the saints through the ages have waited upon God early in the day. As more than one poet has said, to do so is to set life's sails for the day's voyage. Whatever the figure of speech, we know that we give our souls an advantage if we set our minds on the holy, the just and the pure.

The morning news is not likely to perform this service, nor is the drive-time radio voice. Neither can we feel sure that the first message on Twitter, the Internet or the telephone will be one of God and goodness. We must do what uncommon good sense would tell us to do: choose the right soul fare early. If we do, the good will draw still more of its own kind to us. And when the less worthy comes, we will be better equipped to reject it. In fact, we may in time come to a place of spiritual maturity where we reject that which is less worthy without even realizing it—just as at some other point in our pilgrimage the mind gravitated to the cheap, the immoral, or the bitter and resentful without our fully knowing it.

The same rules apply to our intellectual fare. There's an abundance of good intellectual fare available, but because of the prevalence of the mediocre and the corrupting we have to know where to find it. Pornography has become a bane of our time, touching lives that were previously out of its reach because it has become as available and as private as the Internet or the cell phone. Then there's also reading and viewing and discussion material that isn't corrupting but is addictive because it's the path of least resistance. It's easier to gossip than to think, easier to rant than to reason, easier to be confirmed in our prejudices than to listen to another person's point of view. And we're especially susceptible to that which is mediocre. The mediocre is comfortable; it doesn't challenge us intellectually, and it is familiar. It's like that old shoe; we can slip it on without struggle or discomfort. And we don't need to condemn ourselves because most of it is not measurably evil; it's just not very demanding. The mediocre will stunt our mental growth but the process is so gradual that there's no pain of conscience.

One thing is sure. If we form the habit of mediocre intellectual fare, our minds will draw ever more such mediocrity to themselves. The supply seems endless! And as time goes by, the mediocre taste deteriorates until that which is rather crude and senseless qualifies as mediocre. In time we come to a place where we not only do not desire the intellectually stimulating and challenging, we aren't able even to recognize it.

While this state of mind is serious for any person, it is especially so for those of us who name ourselves Christians, since we are called to love the Lord our God with our whole mind. But it is flat-out tragic for the Christian preacher or teacher, because we set the standard for the people who look to us for leadership.

> We are more vulnerable to distraction when we are unclear about just what the real task or subject is. As long as we are uncertain on that point, the more problematic distraction becomes, for detour turns into destination.
>
> *David J. Kalas, senior pastor, First United Methodist Church, Green Bay, Wisconsin*

I am not calling for intellectualized preaching. The preacher who seeks to prove his or her scholarship is soon talking to an exceedingly small audience. The common people heard Jesus gladly because they could understand him. John and Charles Wesley reached the miners, the servants, the street sweepers and the illiterate of England because they made their preaching and singing accessible. But never for lack of thought and creativity.

So we need terribly to establish a mindset of the good and the holy, the kind of thinking that will draw to itself material of imaginative, intellectual and spiritual quality. This is not so much a matter of censors that shut some things out—though certainly that is important—but of sensors that know what to admit. You and I are able to determine to a surprising degree the kind of distractions that will seek residence within us. But we will have to be intentional in training both our sensors and our censors. It won't just happen.

Training Our Selective Instincts

When a municipality contemplates installing new traffic lights on a given corner, they first make a study of the traffic patterns: how many cars go in particular directions at given hours of the day and night? How much left-turn activity is there and at what times? With such knowledge the engineers are ready to develop a traffic control system. If we're serious about what is happening to our thinking and if we hope to control the traffic of both productive and destructive distractions, we need to analyze our thought patterns. When are we most distracted in destructive ways? While we're in our automobile, alone with our thoughts? While listening to the car radio? When we sit down to our computer or engage our iPhone? While in particular conversations?

What kinds of reading stimulate a preacher's thinking and creativity? Since a preacher is a communicator, the preacher does well to read that which will aid this skill. I urge reading some good poetry, because poets specialize in the use of words, and words are a preacher's basic tool. Some modern poets tend to be obscure; this troubles me because I think that we should aim to be understood rather than exclusive.[4] I also encourage my preaching students to read good novels (not hammock reading, though there's probably a place for that, too), because novels and short stories help one see character development and to understand the principle of plot. Character development is important because we're talking to people, not machines, and because the Bible is packed solid with interesting people. And plot is crucial because a sermon should always have a plot. Whether its structure is line-by-line exposition, narrative or a series of points, there should be a plot. I happen also to like familiar essays and good biographies. And lest you wonder, I read the Bible with care every morning. I first read it from Genesis to Revelation when I was eleven years old and have done so many times since, and I still find something new every day.

Be selective about your reading, because you can't possibly read everything that comes your way. We can't even read all the books within our profession. Don't feel obligated to read a book because it's currently popular or because a friend recommends it. Some years ago I stumbled upon a rule that I've never forgotten, though I don't know who said it. It goes something like this: Always remember when you pick up a book to read that in doing so you are, for that period of time, rejecting all the other books in the world in order to read this one.

And what of our physical and emotional state? Perhaps there are times when we're so physically exhausted that everything distracts, but especially the sad and the shoddy. So, too, when we are emotionally distraught: try as we will to concentrate on a sermon that must be written or a lecture prepared, the mind is drawn toward themes of defeat, despair, betrayals, past hurts and petty behavior.

Some of these problems may call for a heart-to-heart visit with a friend who is a good listener or perhaps guidance from a good counselor. But we can handle most of the questions I've raised by changing some of our patterns of work and rest and by being much more discerning of our own thinking, and after that much more intentional in dealing with our personal "traffic patterns."

Some Basic Guidelines

You may be more comfortable classifying all distractions as bad. It's easier to spot the enemy if he can be identified by the color of his uniform. But there are times when we need to be distracted. When that which occupies our minds is trivial, unproductive, constitutionally tedious or even downright destructive, a distraction is to our benefit. And as I said earlier, distractions are sometimes the growing edge of life. We need therefore to have some general guidelines to help us avoid distractions that deter us and use those that will bless us.

The mariner counts on a compass that knows true north. Christians begin with their commitment to God as revealed in Jesus Christ. "God's goal," the apostle Paul said, "is for us to become mature adults—to be fully grown, measured by the standard of the fullness of Christ" (Eph 4:13). Here then is a basic question for the Christian living in a world of distractions: Does this area of thinking lead to my "growing up" in Christ? If I follow a particular course of thought, will it bring me closer to the fullness of Christ?

Obviously this standard rules out the distractions that are clearly base and morally corrupting—which means not only that which is sexually seductive but also that which makes us envious, resentful or jealous. It may be easier to deal with the former than with the latter, because the latter is not so obvious.

But we need to attend to that which is not so obvious. In the pursuit of the Christlike life, spiritual contentment is as much a hazard as salacious thought. We too easily measure ourselves by the lives of others—and, of course, by others as we see them, not necessarily as they are. But the biblical standard is a life that takes on the image and fullness of Christ. This means that we can't be content with mediocrity—because there's nothing mediocre in being Christlike. God's intention for us is high beyond our imagining and high beyond our comfort zone. Thus we judge the thought—the distraction—that comes to us by this question: Does this incline me toward Christ or away from him? If I pursue this thought, what will it do to my mind and spirit? Back to the image of the mariner: What does the compass say about the direction of this thought?

I am not appealing for a painfully pious life. Jesus didn't receive all of those social invitations (for which the Pharisees despised him) because of the seriousness of his manner. Laughter followed him. Children came to him because they sensed that he was fun to be with, not because he was foreboding. He came to bring life abundant, not life diminished. And that's the point. Our Lord is the Lord of fullness. As I read his parables, I sense that those who listened to him had to keep their sense of humor alert or they would be frowning when they should have been chuckling. Sometimes the disciples tried to make Jesus worry as much as they did and live within the boundaries of prejudice that crippled their lives. But there was nothing mediocre in him. He lived the life triumphant and he invited his followers to do the same.

So it is that we should test the multiple voices that solicit us each day. We have a direct, no-nonsense question: Will this "distraction" lead to more life or to less? Will it bless me so that I will bless others or will it diminish me so that I will enjoy diminishing others? Does the thought to which I'm giving attention in my reading, listening or cogitating lead to the fullness of life or to a smallness and a cor-

rupting of life? Our Lord Christ is the true north for our spiritual and
intellectual compass.

In one form or another we need at the beginning of each day to
tell God our situation. In the course of this day, you and I will receive
more solicitations than anyone can count. At times they will come
to us so rapidly, so pell-mell, that we will hardly know where one
ends and the other begins. Some of these solicitations will make us
more complete persons in the likeness of God's Son, and some will
do just the opposite, though at times quite subtly. We need to keep
our spiritual compasses in good repair.

It is with such an attitude and such a prayer that we should start
each day. And obviously, we do well to renew this prayer as the hours
of the day unfold.

SMELLING LIKE SHEEP

A Catholic priest friend told me that he received a word from Pope Francis: "Priests are supposed to smell like sheep." I love that. It means that our "office" is not a room filled with books but it's where our people are. We're not to smell like libraries but sheep.

That's not to diminish the need for thoughtful study. Far from it! But if we are going to have something to say to people in our churches who struggle with internal and external challenges that would likely make our eyes bug out, we better make sure our preaching shines the truth of God's Word on their world.

To that end I've developed the pattern of writing sermons at Starbucks. As distracting as a coffee shop, restaurant, park (on a really pleasant day) or other venue may be, the overwhelming benefit is that every time I look up I see people God loves. I see people laughing, crying, hurting, busy and likely living without any notion of God's presence in their everyday lives. Lord, let my heart break like yours for the people around me! I think the "distractions" are making me a better preacher.

Paul Clines, executive pastor, First United Methodist Church, Houston, Texas (Westchase Campus)

6

EXCELLENCE AS A COUNTERFORCE

So how does the preacher or teacher cope with the times in which we live? How do we get the attention of people who live in the midst of distraction—and sometimes, worse yet, when they seem to court still more distraction? How do we hold their attention for ten minutes, or twenty-five, or perhaps even an hour? For that matter, how do we get small pieces of their attention in the midst of the sights, sounds and subtleties that keep taking them from us?

Several years ago an investment firm became memorable for a commercial in which its spokesman promised potential clients, "They make money the old-fashioned way. They earn it." Let me start in something of that mood by recommending another concept that may seem old-fashioned and not at all geared to our pace of living; let me make a case for the potential that exists in excellence. I like to believe that our souls are still susceptible to that which is above average. I submit, at the least, that it's worth a try. It may come as such a surprise that we will embrace it with the excitement that comes with discovery.

Certainly excellence has captured our hearts in some areas of twenty-first-century life. Take computers, for instance. In 1962 a computer began processing data in a laboratory at the Massachusetts Institute of Technology to assist with biomedical research. It measured about eight square feet, had a thousand bytes of memory, and sold for $43,600. Fifty years later almost any middle school student has an iPhone that measures five by two inches, has sixteen billion bytes of memory, and sells for $199. The automobile's progress isn't quite that dramatic, but we take its improved benefits for granted. In an earlier day the attendant at the service station always lifted the hood to see if we needed to add a quart of oil before the next thousand-mile change—and we often did. Now no one looks under the hood, and we wouldn't think of changing oil before less than three thousand miles, if then.

Medical science has also enjoyed dramatic gains. Roughly half a century ago cataract surgery meant days of absolute immobility and an extended hospital stay. Today the patient comes to the eye clinic in the morning, has the intricate procedure without discomfort, and stops for lunch at a restaurant on the way home. In another day the attentive parish pastor knew there would be opportunities over several days to call on the patient who had undergone surgery. Now the odds are good that the same surgery will be an outpatient experience with no time in the hospital.

We take such progress for granted, and perhaps aren't even properly impressed—at least, not until we experience the benefits personally. We live in a time when change is the norm, and we reserve judgment as to whether or not any given change is in truth progress.

The Problem of Measurement

But once we move out of the technical and physical world, the signs of progress that lead to excellence are not so easy to observe. We can put words on paper at a speed that Shakespeare could not have imagined possible, but not many students of language will suggest that the words we write compare with those of Shakespeare. We have audio systems that bring music to the millions, but how many composers do we have whose work merits such excellent delivery? And more directly to the point of this book: Is our generation producing saints at a per capita rate that compares with some periods in the past? Or a pragmatic question: We are geniuses at developing instruments of mass destruction, but are we developing peacemakers of such excellence that they can protect us from our ability to destroy?

Of course, I'm asking us to compare apples and potatoes. It's easy to measure excellence in physical matters. We can count megabytes; we can demonstrate the number of miles traveled per gallon of fuel; statistics show how twenty-first-century longevity compares with what our grandparents knew. It's not as simple, however, to "prove" the comparative excellence of poets and playwrights, of artists and composers and architects. Some avoid considering such judgment by saying that it's all a matter of taste. To a degree, perhaps, though history has a way of winnowing out a good deal of life's chaff. And since we have become experts in debunking, we may have lost our capacity for recognizing saints.

Nevertheless, something in us is hungry for excellence. And even when we don't know how to describe what we're looking for, we seem to recognize excellence when we see it. Some of us fear that we're losing our taste for excellence because we see so little of it. In a culture where everyone has fifteen minutes of fame and where reputations are the product of a good publicity agent we may cast our vote for excellence with a shrug of the shoulders. Still, we want excellence. We know there is a difference—or ought to be—between what is average and what is extraordinary. And if pressed, we seem eventually to see the difference between synthetic popularity and true quality.

In this discussion I confess a prejudice. It is for me an element of doctrine. As surely as I believe that we humans are made in the image of God, I believe that we possess an innate hunger for excellence, as well as for truth and integrity and holiness of life. I know full well that living in a fallen world has scarred our judgment. I realize that our taste has been misshapen by sin. But I am satisfied that there is still enough of Eden residual in each soul that we want to be better than we are. The culture may seek to coarsen us for its own benefit, but something in us refuses to settle for the sod as long as there are stars.

It is part of the calling of the Christian preacher and teacher to keep Eden alive in the human soul. As we seek to save the soul, we should respect the mind and body in which the soul resides. Our aim, after all, is to appeal to that which is best in every human creature. We ought therefore to raise and clarify the definition of what is best.

The Search for Excellence

G. K. Chesterton is famously quoted as saying, "The Christian ideal has not been tried and found wanting. It has been found difficult; and left untried." Sometimes one has the same feeling about excellence in general. Several lesser options have much more appeal, especially that which is new or "cutting-edge" or "groundbreaking": choose your adjective but recognize that the appeal is novelty and recognize that novelty is not the same thing as excellence. Often it is only a poor substitute.

Excellence proves itself not by the sheen of newness but by the scars of survival. A product, a person, a poem, a symphony or a rule of life shows its excellence by living on and by looking better with the passing of time. Unfortunately, the appeal of most training events for clergy is in the new and the clever. We are like the person who happily seeks out an unproved wonder drug rather than taking on the discipline of a change in habits. It is now a century ago that E. M. Bounds chastised American Protestantism by writing, "The Church is looking for better methods; God is looking for better men." The only thing that has changed since Bounds is that we now publicize our method search more persuasively and offer new methods in greater variety.

Fortunately, I am encouraged by the students I see in my classes. Perhaps they are in fact what I sometimes tell them they are: the best students one could find anywhere. True, I wish some of them had a better literary background, and I confess that I'm not on their page in church music. But I'm altogether certain that the graduates I saw this past spring are superior to my class from a long generation ago. And they'd better be, because they're going out to tougher assignments than we faced in those days.

But I want to be sure they know the difference between fluff and substance, between cleverness and excellence. Now and again I see a restaurant try to lift itself to success by reinventing its ambiance, introducing a new menu and rearranging its tables when quite clearly what it needs is better food. Often churches and preachers follow the same course. No wonder such efforts end in disappointment.

I confess that excellence may seem a naive recommendation for our culture. It is now more than half a century that television has been the primary educator in America. Humor has been replaced by shock. An audience knows it is time to laugh not because of the timing of the master storyteller or the punch line, but because a crude word or phrase has been spoken. The evening newscast a generation ago concluded with a thoughtful analysis, an oral editorial. Mind you, it was not a ranting, doctrinaire declaration but an appeal to thoughtful analysis. In the world of television drama there were programs that stimulated the mind while entertaining; one thinks of a time when plays like *Twelve Angry Men, Requiem for a Heavyweight, The Miracle Worker* and *Judgment at Nuremberg* were all written expressly for television—mind you, for commercial television.

Because of television's broad impact, it can reasonably be called the primary shaper of public taste. It is often masterful in its use of visual images; for this we can be grateful. It sometimes claims to reflect the public taste. But by this time it's clear that it has rather shaped public taste. What will happen as variations of the Internet take over is yet to be seen, but there is little reason to think that it will be an improvement.

Is Excellence Obsolete?

Which is to say that the common taste has been in decline for roughly two generations. Can the beleaguered pastor hope to make a place in such a culture by seeking for greater pulpit excellence? I am altogether certain that humans respond to quality when it becomes a viable, available option. But of course our taste—whether we're talking about food, books, entertainment, art or character—depends very much on the diet on which we've been raised.

Peter Gomes, the late Plummer professor of Christian morals at Harvard University, recalls that in his high school days the reading of "great literature" was "understood to be part of our moral as well as our literary education," and such reading always meant "much time discussing and debating, but it was a part of our moral education, and no opportunity was lost, ever, to discuss the ambiguities of motivation, the limits of human freedom, the relationship of fate to free will, and the conflicts of the vices and virtues in the construction of the human experience."[1] I wonder if high school graduates in Gomes's time were better prepared to listen with depth of attention than are many college and university graduates of more recent times. Today colleges concentrate more on training students to make a living in their chosen vocations, with significantly less attention to moral and ethical issues. Yet life is made up of moral and ethical decisions. Not just in international relations but in business, sports, the family and church.

This has implications for those of us who minister in the church. If those in the pews are not accustomed by way of high school or college classes in literature, history and civics to think seriously about the meaning of human conduct, the preacher is a voice crying in the wilderness when he or she speaks of sin, conscience and basic moral conduct—to say nothing of salvation and godly living. Many people are concerned because the Bible is no longer taught in public schools. That's just the most obvious part of the matter. National columnist Ross Douthat points to a respected survey of high school students that reveals that their definition of a moral person "means being the kind of person that other people will like." By such a standard, Douthat goes on to say, "niceness is the highest ethical standard, popularity the most important goal, and high self-esteem the surest sign of sanctity."[2] I fear that many Christians are satisfied with that definition of character and morals, not because they are shallow and certainly not because they don't care, but because the influences of our daily culture creep into our moral judgments.

Our nineteenth-century ancestors believed with Longfellow that

Life is real! Life is earnest!
And the grave is not its goal.[3]

But many of the people to whom we preach have never felt the challenge to ask themselves about life or the grave. Mind you, to be human is to think at times about both life and grave, but the context for such thinking doesn't get much encouragement in our culture. We run from such subjects rather than wrestling with them. No wonder, then, if the preacher sometimes thinks the congregation is more attentive to the children's talk than to the sermon that comes later.

When the students in my preaching classes read some of the classical sermons from the mid-nineteenth and early twentieth centuries they sometimes complain that if they quoted from poets or essayists of another generation as those preachers did, their congregations wouldn't know who they were talking about. I suspect (indeed, I fear) they are right. Shall the preacher decide therefore to limit quotations to contemporaries—headline contemporaries, to be more specific?

I submit that it's at just such points that we should aim for excellence. Mind you, the reference we quote should be valuable not for the person who said it, but for the quality of the statement itself. If a statement is powerful in its truth and in the language in which it is conveyed, it is worth quoting, whether it comes from Shakespeare, Yogi Berra or "seventeenth-century anonymous." And on the other hand, if the saying itself is trivial, no name can give it any real significance. At the same time, however, the subject of the quotation must matter to the hearer. If it does the quotation will give force to the subject even as the subject makes the quotation a matter of interest.

Without a doubt our contemporary culture is fascinated with itself. This isn't unique to this generation, but it has reached new proportions. A college and seminary graduate advised me several years ago that she wasn't interested in reading the church fathers of the fourth and fifth centuries because she didn't believe anything of any worth had been written except in the last ten years. Hers was an extreme view (I hope!) but it simply exaggerates what a great many in our time believe; they have little interest in what people have done or said in the past. This is a serious issue for those of us who believe in the historical Christian faith and whose singular document is a book whose parts date for millennia.

So let us seek for excellence, wherever it may be found. If the source is a familiar one so that the listener responds with a light of recognition, all the better. But seek for that which is good and persuasive simply because it is excellent. Whether the cartoonist said it through Charlie Brown or the poet said it through Robert Browning's Pippa, if quality is there, employ it.

The Excellence of the Scriptures

Needless to say, this is all the more true where the Scriptures are involved. If our populace is becoming scripturally illiterate, we should by no means acquiesce by using the Scriptures less. Rather, quote more carefully, quote with explanation of context, quote with sympathy for those who know little, and quote with passion. Scripture will assert itself by virtue of its inherent authority if only we give it a reasonable chance to be heard.

In truth, I venture that increasingly the language of Scripture will be the only common language within our congregations. Our population now lives in such culturally independent worlds that one person's cliché is another person's revelation. Half a century ago popular music could have a "hit parade"; today there is no such thing as popular music—only popularity within a variety of subdivisions that range from classic country and western to progressive rock.

In like manner, the newsstands have long forgotten popular weekly magazines that everyone recognized. One used to be able to find *Liberty*, the *Saturday Evening Post* or *Colliers* in the barber shop, the doctor's waiting room or the pastor's study; we have no such crossover publications in our day. The church is becoming like the African nations where dozens of tribal languages are spoken but the legislative sessions are in English; the people who gather for worship each week speak technical, artistic, economic, pragmatic or essential English during the week but have a common language on Saturday or Sunday—the Holy Scriptures. That is, we have such a common language if we use it.

For this very pragmatic reason, at the least, the effective preacher-pastor needs to be a biblical preacher. I hope pastors see the Bible as the inspired Word of God. But if there is one who, pragmatically, simply wants to be heard and understood each Sunday, then he or she should work with the document that is the common speech of the complex variety that sit in the pews. Illustrations from sports, science, biographies, economics, nature and current headlines speak only to those segments of the audience for whom this is the primary interest. For others who are outside that interest, the reference may be not only meaningless but an irritant. But the document that is common to all these people—or that surely ought to be—is the book of their faith, their holy heritage, the Bible. In a time of increasing biblical illiteracy, the pastor must lay new claim to the Scriptures and preach them with more depth, conviction and excellence than ever before.

I'm sure my counsel seems counterintuitive to some. Conventional wisdom advises us to estimate the taste of the people and aim for that level; thus if the common denominator is tacky, learn how to be tacky (it isn't difficult). I contend that there is always a market for excellence. Further, though that market seems submerged by prevailing mediocrity, the mediocrity itself makes people restless for something better. You and I should be ready with the something better.

In the past two decades Fleming Rutledge may have preached in a greater variety of American pulpits than anyone I know of, beginning with her own Episcopal heritage and extending to both mainline and evangelical churches. "Our entire middle-class culture is in danger of losing its soul," she writes. "American values are being shaped to an unprecedented degree by inane movies pitched to the lowest common adolescent denominator, by music videos, by soap operas, and it's all happening almost imperceptibly, so that Christians are able to discern the difference between what is Christian and what is merely cultural only by exercising perpetual vigilance."[4] If that be so—and I'm painfully sure that it is—then the Christian preacher and teacher have an obligation to both God and culture to be counterintuitive and to push the cause of excellence in the morass of cultural deterioration.

It Can Happen Here

We have a precedent of hope, and it comes from an era worse than ours. While eighteenth-century England, with Oliver Goldsmith, Samuel Johnson, Alexander Pope and David Garrick (to name a few), had no shortage of talent, the mass of the population was illiterate, economically destitute and morally base. The general populace didn't have the variety of distractions that we experience today, but they were consumed by what they did have. A sociologist might have concluded that even if God loved the masses, there was no hope for them—certainly not for any admirable pattern of living.

But John and Charles Wesley thought otherwise. Their vigorous preaching moved into the most hopeless areas, with street preaching and field preaching and services outside the mine entrances. One would expect that in working with such congregants the Wesley brothers would have sought the lowest common denominator. Not so. Charles Wesley packed doctrine and Scripture into his hymns, and John's sermons, though always aimed at being accessible, were never superficial.

More than that, John Wesley intended for his converts to become an intelligent citizenry. As Oscar Sherwin has put it, "Wesley helped to democratize learning." For him, Sherwin writes, "evangelical conversion had as a sequel the overcoming of illiteracy in the individual."[5] Wesley proudly declared himself "a man of one Book," the Bible, but he was an Oxford scholar through and through, and he wanted his converts to know many books. The fourteenth edition of Encyclopedia Britannica says of John Wesley that none in the eighteenth century "did so much to create a taste for good reading and to supply it with books at the lowest prices."[6] Wesley did so by producing condensed versions of dozens of classics, from Milton's *Paradise Lost* to Bunyan's *Pilgrim's Progress*. Who would have dared to think that once-illiterate colliers and factory workers would read such books, to say nothing of Wesley's *Concise History of England*? Counterintuitive indeed!

I suspect I am in danger of seeming elitist. The furthest thing from it. The elitist is someone who finds satisfaction in knowing (or experiencing, or enjoying, or eating) what others do not. My position is the opposite: the better something is, the more people I hope will be reached by it. The best art, whether graphic or literary, is accessible. After all, if an insight or a conviction cannot be understood, it is an absurd waste for both the producer and the receiver. But the music, the sermon, the lesson should stimulate both the mind and the spirit, and they should lead worshipers closer to the mind of God rather than to that which is shoddy, imitative and carelessly prepared. The people of God deserve the best that is available. Excellence should be the norm.

I am speaking, yes, of intellectual and artistic excellence, but far, far more of spiritual excellence. Our worship and our preaching have been too content with saving souls and keeping them moderately alive when our New Testament assignment is to produce saints, men and women who seek to fulfill "the standard of the fullness of Christ"

(Eph 4:13). John promised the first generation of believers that "it hasn't yet appeared what we will be" (1 Jn 3:2). The expectations were wonderfully high. The Christian life was seen as full of promise and therefore full of challenge. It was not one of many philosophies, not just another product in the marketplace of Athens philosophers, but a whole new way of life, a way of holy excellence. Who can imagine what God wants us to be and what therefore we might become, the apostles said to a world of slaves, shopkeepers, day laborers and marginalized women and children!

What the early church said to its lost world we must learn to say to our distracted world. We must give our generation a call to the excellence that is the essence of life in Jesus Christ. And we must do so with an excellence of thought and delivery worthy of the subject that is our trust.

LISTENING IN AN AGE OF DISTRACTION

"If [a person] were happy, he would be the more so, the less he was diverted, like the Saints and God."[7] This observation was articulated by Blaise Pascal, a seventeenth-century French mathematician, scientist, philosopher and theologian, long before diversions like Facebook, Twitter and the smartphone were ever conceived. Distraction is certainly not a novel temptation for the human race, but the intensity of its lure has amplified, especially over the past few decades.

The rigors of the preaching life make escape through distraction even more appealing. The preacher is called to the painstaking focus required for the practice of listening to the will of God for the people of God through the Word of God.

Since distraction is more accessible and affordable than ever, at the fingertip of our cell phone, iPad or iPod, the preacher can too easily avoid the challenge of long listening and deep reflection. Habitual avoidance by way of distraction creates a behavioral pattern in the preacher that is not easily overcome.

The best preachers, then, are the best listeners. Listening happens most when distractions are at their least. I have a friend who cannot keep his fingers off his cell phone, even while I voice my significant struggles and stresses. Once I discovered that listening is not my friend's forte and distraction is, I began withholding from him the hopes and happenings of my life. God is likely frustrated with distracted preachers, much like I am with my cell-phone-focused friend. How can the preacher receive from God something of substance to say by the time Sunday rolls around if the preacher is too distracted to listen the rest of the week?

The preacher courageous enough to swim against the current will remediate distraction to foster listening. The potential reward at the end of the swim is perspective on the intersection of the biblical text with the contemporary context, sermonic creativity and clarity and, best of all, the presence and power of God. Life-transforming sermons today are proclaimed by preachers who shut up distractions in order to listen up to the God who speaks up.

Lenny Luchetti, professor of proclamation and Christian ministry, Wesley Seminary, Indiana Wesleyan University

7

CREATIVITY AND DISTRACTION

Ha!

George Bernard Shaw said, "Few people think more than two or three times a year. I have made an international reputation for myself by thinking once or twice a week." That sounds easy enough as Shaw addresses the matter in his curmudgeonly fashion, but the every-Sunday preacher soon learns that "thinking once or twice a week" isn't so simple.

During the ten years that I was the senior minister at the First United Methodist Church in Madison, Wisconsin, I occasionally crossed paths with a man who had been my communications professor some years before. On several occasions he enjoyed telling me that it was impossible for someone to have something new and worthwhile to say every Sunday for some forty-seven or forty-eight Sundays of the year. He wasn't a member of my congregation so I didn't take his comment personally, but I prodded myself with it. Is every pastor carrying an impossible assignment? Is the week-by-week task beyond anyone's creative capacity? Consider that the great Hebrew prophets spoke only when the Spirit came upon them. Can we expect someone to receive a word from the Lord week after

Hm. Is it biblical to preach weekly?

week, year after year, as an assignment to hand in at eight-thirty and eleven a.m.?

This book operates from a prejudice of sorts. While I hope it has value for all preachers and teachers (and, indeed, in some measure for twenty-first-century people in general), my thinking returns repeatedly to the parish pastor, that person who steps into the same pulpit forty or more Sundays of the year and looks out at essentially the same body of people. I filled that role for nearly forty years in churches in Wisconsin and in Cleveland, Ohio, and I look back on those years with pride and gratitude. With repentance, too, you can be sure, because I know full well that I was never as wise, as capable and as godly as I wanted to be. But pride and gratitude are my dominant moods; pride because I think being a pastor is as high a calling as one can aspire to, and gratitude because I was privileged to have such an assignment. *? How old is this guy?*

In the twenty-five years since then I have preached in several hundred churches and in a vast variety of sacred and secular occasions. This is a worthy ministry in its own right, but it lacks the continuity that informs and empowers—and challenges!—the every-Sunday pastor. On the one hand, almost anyone can come up with one or half-a-dozen reasonably good sermons in the course of a year, and one can count on it that the novelty of the guest speaker will give a certain vigor and immediacy to what is said. On the other hand, however, the guest speaker is always just that—a guest, or perhaps a novelty—while the every-week preacher has the authority of presence and familiarity.

Nevertheless, it is that familiarity and presence that put a special burden on the every-week preacher. Since it is the same voice, the same face and pretty much the same gestures being employed, the sermon content itself has to be thoughtful enough that the regular listeners can't turn off their attention because they think (indeed, they're rather sure) they've heard this before, or at least something rather much like it.

The Necessity of Creativity

Eugene Peterson has been honest in describing a period in his more-than-thirty-year pastorate when he was disillusioned by the lack of intellectual and spiritual hunger in his people. He realized that he had to come to terms with his congregation "just as they were: their less-than-developed emotional life, their lack of intellectual curiosity, their complacent acceptance of a world of consumption and diversion, their seemingly peripheral interest in God." In the process, he writes, "I was becoming a pastor who wasn't in a hurry."[1]

That not-being-in-a-hurry is a crucial phrase. It isn't a confession of defeat, nor is it a resignation to the idea that things will always be as they are now. Rather, it is the recognition that the pastoral ministry is a marathon, not a sprint. There are times of sprinting, but they should be practiced with caution lest one forget that the journey is a very long one.

It is in this matter of not being in a hurry that creativity becomes a primary issue to the preacher. The issue is of two parts. For one, it isn't possible to put creativity on a time schedule. I believe with Samuel Johnson that "a man may write at any time if he will set himself doggedly to it," and I follow that rule whether I'm working on a sermon, a book or a challenging email. But there is no formula to "doggedly" and no timetable. The creative muse doesn't answer to some mystical incantation. And if you think you've found a can't-fail method, you'll discover otherwise before long.

All of us can find ways, however, to make ourselves more hospitable to the creative impulse. We learn that we're more productive in some settings than in others. We're probably better at particular parts of the day or night. We learn that there is some connection between our motor activity and creativity—for some it's a walk in a park, for another a leaning back in a chair; for some it's writing in longhand and for others it's hovering over a computer or even an ancient typewriter. Some learn how often they need a break, and some can hardly imagine creativity happening without a cup of coffee or a cold beverage near at hand. We learn little secrets about ourselves and the creativity that is sometimes our ally and sometimes our playful, elusive visitor.

But mostly we find that we can't be in a hurry. If you want to be creative in November, begin turning yourself that way in April. Read the books that quicken your thinking. They may or may not be best-sellers (some of the best in my experience have been little known, and I'm not sure whether it is the content that impressed itself on me or whether it was simply a matter of the right book at the right time). Conversations with the right people are like special, living books, but these too are unpredictable. Some quite successful people are not very helpful because they may not be introspective enough to understand their own method, if any. Some of the most exciting conversations in my pastoral days were with elderly people who were using their solitude to ruminate. Such persons have a way of turning a commonplace matter on its head, so that suddenly the common becomes intriguing, and the conversation seems like a visitation by the Holy Spirit.

My November-April reference is my way of saying that we must invest regularly and at length in the soul and mind if we expect to find something awaiting us when resources are needed. And while much can be said for filing and organizing the best of what we read and hear and experience, don't expect your organized file to be all that helpful.

The mind is of course the most marvelous of computers, imaginative beyond any estimate. But it lives by its own rules, and it isn't always sympathetic to the rules we impose on it. That's what makes the mind so creative. It connects insights and data that don't necessarily fit in the same file drawer. This is what makes the material exciting! The purely logical course of an idea ends up where the reader or listener can see it coming, while the creative one catches us off-guard. I suspect that this is what novelists mean when they say they don't know how their story will end until they see what their characters do. But the more material the mind has to work with, the more creative possibilities that will come our way.

Creativity Under Pressure

Still, however, time is a factor. If we do nothing but read and attend seminars, we may come out sounding like a compendium of quotations and stories. We need time simply to think. This time must be concentrated and directed, yes, because we have a theme and almost surely a deadline. But we need to leave the reins loose enough that the horse may carry us down a more fascinating road than we had planned.

I don't want to encourage desultory habits that may already be a pitfall in your creative path, but if I am to be honest I must confess that sometimes creativity works remarkably under pressure. This is probably an extension of Dr. Johnson's famous rule: "Depend upon it, Sir, when a man knows he is to be hanged in a fortnight, it concentrates his mind wonderfully." When the deadline hour is near, it can either stimulate creativity beyond one's best hopes or it can convince one to go into a less strenuous occupation than preaching.

Still, I think of a time at a church breakfast when a telephone call advised us that the preacher of the morning had taken suddenly ill.

As a guest at the banquet, I was drafted to pinch-hit. I stepped outside for fresh air and solitude, pondered that my hanging was less than half-an-hour away, and noticed that the church across the street was one for Latter-day Saints. Something in my soul reminded me that in some way or another, we're always living in latter days and that saints are always needed. I knew then that my text was with Noah and that the mark of every latter-day saint is that he or she is contrary to the times and available therefore to the purposes of God. To my surprise and wonder, the basic sermon content was already well in hand. I preached it half an hour later, then put it on paper when I returned home the following week.

But even after such an experience, I don't recommend that we count on such instant creativity. I remind myself that the reason the idea found form and content so quickly is because of the decades of reading and listening that were at work in my soul when I stood looking across the street. And for that matter, the only reason the quote from Samuel Johnson appears in the previous paragraph is because I heard it and made it part of my person many years ago. How long ago, I don't know, but long enough that it reinforces my point: if you want to have creativity in November, begin preparing yourself in April.

This is one factor in the relationship between time and creativity. The other is the people who hear us preach and teach. The longer the period of time over which they hear us, the more creative we're compelled to be. Our greatest obligation is not to the fringe person we hope to win or the newcomer that gladdens our soul but the people who faithfully give us their attention week after week, year after year. A United Methodist bishop recalls how a member of a church described what they hoped for in a new pastor: "We do not need a really great preacher at our little church—but after the worship service, I don't want to feel like I wasted my time."

This doesn't seem like an unreasonable request but we understand why the faithful parishioner spoke it. Too many sermons have something of the flavor of a prepackaged frozen dinner: there aren't many made-from-scratch evidences. Mind you, creativity seems to come much harder for some people. Nature has not distributed creativity in equal measure. There's no doubt that fresh ideas come rather easily and readily to some, while it's a slow, painful process for others.

Nevertheless, I can't help feeling that preachers sometimes give up the creative search too soon. The Internet is readily available, and various subscription agencies offer enticing homiletical packages. The responsibilities of the week are long and the preparation time between two Sundays is short. So the pastor grabs what is easily at hand. As it happens, what is at hand may be more professional than what the pastor himself would prepare. Nevertheless, it lacks the authenticity and the sense of personal passion that comes with a sermon that "belongs" to the preacher. Still more important, processed material rarely imparts the excitement that comes when an idea springs forth after the preacher has wrestled with the Scriptures until a light has come on in the soul.

A preacher would do well to set up this inner standard: that every sermon will have in it some insight, some personal awe, some wonder of Scripture that is for him or her quite new—and therefore quite exciting. Obviously I'm not suggesting insights outside scriptural and doctrinal integrity; rather, I'm calling for insights that make the familiar idea come alive with a new glory, like a suit or dress that reveals a personality not formerly apparent in the wearer. The longer a preacher serves a given congregation, the more important it is that this kind of creativity mark the pulpit fare. This is as much for the preacher's sake as for the congregation's because of what it does for the preacher's own soul. And for self-confidence, too. It's true that pride is a deadly sin to which we clergy are quite susceptible. But self-despising is deadly, too, and self-despising is as much an issue of the self as pride—that is, it causes one to think about the self rather than about better subjects. If there's a place for wholesome pride, it is in the quality we hope to bring to our calling.

I've never met the classic photographer John Szarkowski, but in matters of creativity I recommend him as a model for the preacher— especially the every-Sunday preacher. Szarkowski finds a magic in photography so that lets him "take pictures of the same empty lot for his entire life and never repeat an image." How is this so? Because "once you come to understand the landscape—to respect it, to feel empathy for its subtle moods and attitudes—you begin to appreciate its newness." He has a marvelous phrase. Great photographers, in his judgment, "never suffer the boredom of the expected."[2]

Forgive me, please, while I dare to spell out my point. If an artist-photographer has learned to despise "the boredom of the expected," how much more should a preacher of the gospel despise it? If a congregation thinks two or three minutes into the sermon that they're pretty sure they've heard this before and know therefore what to expect—boredom!—who can blame them for meditating on a subject of their own? And how can we expect otherwise when these people in the pews live in a world of fiercely competing distractions?

I'm asking us preachers to be as excited about our expounding of Scripture as the entomologist is about still another type of beetle, or as the photographer feels about the way the shadows of a September day affect an empty lot. What do I find in the passage of Scripture lying open before me that I've never seen there before? At the minimum I have at least three possible vantage points for viewing a given Scripture: for one, the setting in which that verse came to birth. For another, what it says to me, the messenger, at this particular moment in my life. (We're different persons than we were a year ago and different than we will be next year.) For a third, how this Scripture will sound to the particular body of people who will be present at this moment in their collective history. People heard Scriptures differently on the Sunday after 9/11 and, further back, on the Sunday following John F. Kennedy's assassination. The preacher's creative imagination should be freshly attentive to the unique power of a passage of Scripture at any given time or place, because in the purposes of God no two occasions are the same.

How Can We Be More Creative?

But how can we be more creative? We can start with assurance: Genesis tells us that we are made in the image of God, and God is the ultimate Creator. This suggests that to belittle our creativity is to discredit our biblical heritage. I believe, with Benjamin Disraeli, that a person "is made to create, from the poet to the potter," but I sense from Jesus' parable of the talents that God has distributed creativity with what may sometimes seem like a prejudice. It is said that when Halford Luccock taught preaching at the Yale Divinity School in the first half of the twentieth century he often had accumulated half-a-dozen sermon ideas on the walk from his home to the classroom. Not many are so gifted. What, if anything, can we do to nurture the creative gifts we do have?

To begin with, we need to stop and look. There's a small but telling detail in the story of the call of Moses. As he watched his flocks by Mount Horeb, he saw a bush that was blazing without being consumed. He said, "Let me check out this amazing sight and find out why the bush isn't burning up." And then, the telling sentence: "When the LORD saw that he was coming to look, God called to him out of the bush" (Ex 3:3-4).

I think it is not by chance that the inspired writer said the Lord saw that Moses "was coming to look"—or, as another translation puts it, "that he had turned aside." Moses was a person God could use because he took time to find out the meaning of things. After all, he might logically have fled the scene in fear; I'd understand if he had. Or he could have concluded that this phenomenon was none of his business since he was hired to watch sheep, not bushes, and not even extraordinary bushes. I trust I am not straining the Scripture when I note especially that God called to Moses out of the bush. God spoke to him from the place of Moses' attention. I submit that there are places of fire in every passage of Scripture, if only we will pause to look, and that God will speak to us out of that fire.

Why do we miss them? Sometimes simply because we are preoccupied, and sometimes because we're tired. But also because we've been trained to miss them. We have learned methods of study in seminary or in Bible training conferences, and we have allowed the method to become a boundary of restraint that prevents our moving into unexplored territory. Captive to our method, we look for the things our method has taught us to look for rather than giving ourselves over to holy awe. There is no book like this Book, but because we work with it week after week we unconsciously protect ourselves against its shocking brilliance. Learn some helpful rules, yes; they can give efficiency to your work. But go beyond them. Creativity needs room.

Obviously, part of our creative problem in this world of distractions is that we are caught in such a cacophony of sound that our spiritual and creative ears find it increasingly difficult to hear the music. And because ideas are being thrust upon us from every side—sometimes forcibly!—our powers of distinguishing the excellent from the trivial and mundane are dull.

If we hope to stimulate our creative impulse we'll have to become more selective even while being compelled to consider more possibilities. As for more possibilities, I recommend reading across the centuries. See, for example, why the great philosopher and preacher Jonathan Edwards thought that the millennium might begin in the twentieth century. (We didn't make it!) Or see if you can find any contemporary writing that compares with that of John Donne in his reflections on death and our connectedness to one another: "Any man's death diminishes me"—God knows that our world needs to realize this. And speaking of Donne, find if you can a deeper sense of contrition than when the poet pleads, "Wilt thou forgive those sins through which I run, / And do run still, though still I do deplore?"[3]

We need, too, to read and listen across culture patterns. Most of us are more comfortable with familiar culture patterns and with people whose thinking is like our own. But we can stimulate our thinking by giving attention to those who are different from us—not necessarily as antagonists, because the antagonist is likely to drive us into a defensive posture where we think only more fiercely in our familiar paths—but as individuals who simply approach a subject from a different vantage point. We see the trees and they see the leaves, and that may make all the difference. As we read such a person our creativity is awakened. This is one reason why I enjoy the secular essays of Joseph Epstein.[4]

But especially, if we want to become more creative, we need to become better listeners: better when we read and better when we discuss. We need not only to understand what the other person is saying but also how his or her concepts relate to who we are and how we think. Most of us are inclined in conversation to begin shaping our response to the other person's statements before they've reached the end of their sentence (and let it be said, in your defense and mine, that this may be because some people don't allow a response beyond nodded affirmation). No matter; we need to become intelligent listeners whether we're attending to the printed page, the iPhone or the luncheon visit. Good listening will quicken our creative skills.

And consider the importance of solitude. There is value, certainly, in group prayer, but it is significant that Jesus often went alone to pray. Sometimes we hear best when there's no other voice than ours and that of God's Spirit. Learn to enjoy your own company; treat it with the respect it deserves. As you draw up a list of individuals you ought to join for lunch or coffee, put your own name on the list. Get reacquainted with your own soul. You may discover depths in yourself that, in your hurry, you didn't know were there. It's quite possible that when you take time to get alone with God, God will allow you to get alone with yourself for a while. If you enjoy what you find there, give thanks. If you find instead that this person bearing your name is quite unattractive, remind yourself that the best of saints have had the same experience, and go as they have to the one who makes all things new. Even you. Even me.

Believe me, as we spend undistracted time with our own souls, we find new levels of creativity. I've found that as I've become more conscious of the state of my soul I have preached not only with new depth but also with new compassion. I have sometimes become impatient with the slow, nearly imperceptible growth I've seen in some of my people; then, alone with God and my own soul, I've seen growth in a different light, and I've prayed that I would be as patient with my people as God has been with me.

Those of us who are called to preach and teach and write are compelled to be creative. This has been a demanding assignment from the days of the biblical poets and prophets to the present time. One of those poets complained at length that there was nothing new under the sun, but tens of thousands of his spiritual descendants have labored to prove that there are new ways to reveal what is old. And those who have worked at it devoutly and patiently have found new modes of revealing so that the old takes on strategic new dimensions—just right for this hour and this place.

That's what people have a right to expect when they come to invest twenty minutes or an hour in our presence. Be grateful as you prepare to meet them that you are not alone in your enterprise. The Spirit that was present at creation is your ready, supplicating aide.

ENVISIONING THE MESSAGE

During a week when I'm preparing to preach, I often find myself lying awake at night with visions of the sermon dancing in my head. Even when I turn off the laptop and try to sleep the sermon sometimes refuses to rest, sending me mental pictures of my developing ideas. Scripture passage, illustrations, the points I'd like to make or avoid making.

I'm reminded by those images that come when I close my eyes that we live in a visual age and that on Sunday my congregation will also have visions dancing in their heads as they listen, or try to listen, to the message. I struggle with how to keep them from the distraction of their own imaginations. Where else in their week will they discipline their minds to sit and focus on one person standing still and talking for twenty to thirty minutes? How can I compete with the life of flipping channels, clicking links and touching apps they are accustomed to? I'm afraid the greatest distraction they face during the sermon may simply be lack of stimulation.

Besides capturing and keeping their attention with stories and verbal imagery, I believe firmly that using actual images on the screens in our sanctuary may be my best chance at focusing their concentration on the message I hope to get across. A simple visual metaphor or a snapshot illustrating a personal story can bring to vivid color the words that might have otherwise missed the mark of a scattered stream of thought. Of course, those screens can prove to be a distraction as well if I overuse them, if my slides are too cluttered or too unprofessionally designed, or if technical difficulties frustrate me to the point of visible distraction myself. Still, I believe it's worth the effort and the risk to bring words to life with the occasional well-placed image or phrase that will give those wandering modern minds a visual handle to grab hold of and make them feel at home.

Jessica La Grone, minister of worship, The Woodlands United Methodist Church, The Woodlands (Houston), Texas

8

PACKAGING AND DISTRACTION

My dictionary of quotations says the proverb "You can't tell a book by its cover" was born early in the twentieth century. No doubt that's right, but I'm sure the basic concept existed long before books provided the metaphor. If Jacob's mother, Rebekah, had traveled with him in his search for a wife, she would have given such counsel to her son when he was fascinated by Rachel and overlooked Leah.

We humans have always paid a good deal of attention to packaging. Thus another proverb about outward appearances, "Clothes make the man," dates back to the fifteenth century, but we sense that it is millennia older. I wonder how early it was in human history that people began to feel that the taste of food depended partly on what we now call its "presentation." I have the feeling that this is implied in the story of Abraham hosting the three visitors at the oaks of Mamre (Gen 18:1-8).[1]

Packaging has become a billion-dollar industry in our day. It's a science in its own way. It combines the talents of psychologists, artists and advertising gurus in an attempt to get favorable attention from the shopper. Merchandisers have learned that packaging matters and that specific kinds of packaging appeal to particular types of shoppers. The right kind of packaging gives ambiance to a restaurant, warmth to a gift, winsomeness to a store display.

Contemporary American Christianity has bought into this idea in a big way. From the parking lot to the place of worship, from the greeting to the benediction, the packaging of the gospel has become a major emphasis. This is consistent with our American religious heritage of competition. Because we have freedom of religion rather than a state church, we are part of a religious marketplace, like it or not. But more than that, we compete in the marketplace of ideas and of emotional and spiritual fulfillment. I don't think we can imagine how many places people now turn to in this search. A large percentage wouldn't classify their search as being religious ("spiritual," some would say), but all of human history testifies otherwise. The human soul looks for God often with no idea that God is the point of their search, so they look for God in all kinds of places.

So, yes, packaging matters, because packaging is our first impression of the product. Our current emphasis on religious packaging seems a very long way from the first-century church. Then, believers worshiped where they could—in someone's home, at a riverside or simply where two believers met. There were no advertising campaigns, and probably the only brand symbol was the sign of the fish carefully drawn in the dust.

Neither is religious packaging something new. The sign of the cross probably was several generations in developing after the apostle Paul so bravely named it as our singular identity. Today, however, there is no brand symbol that is more widely known than the cross. Any commercial product would pay the limit to be as universally recognized as the symbol of Christianity. Architecture has also been part of Christianity's packaging genius; one thinks of the classical days of grand gothic structures. Those magnificent buildings said much about the power of the church as an institution as well as the heavenward pull that was effected by the ribbed vault and the flying buttresses. Later, on the American frontier, the simple white-frame building found its place in art, poetry and sentiment. This packaging evokes feelings of a nation with an unadorned hardiness of people and a no-nonsense, natural dignity. Today in hundreds of American urban areas, the storefront church has taken on a peculiar packaging significance. The people of the neighborhood know that this modestly remodeled commercial building belongs to them. I venture that someday some folks will write novels and music about buildings whose natural beauty is hard to find, just as another generation gave us "The Little Brown Church in the Wildwood."

> The grand old cathedrals of Europe had a great wisdom to their design, for even the wandering eye was still invited to focus on God and his word, his glory and his story.
>
> *David J. Kalas*

What happens inside the church also involves packaging. This term may sound crude to those of us who love the liturgy of our particular faith community and the music that is part of our faith. But from the point of view of a secular merchandising expert, the elements of worship are the packaging in which we deliver our faith. There have always been differences in that packaging. American Christianity demonstrated this dramatically when the population moved from the eastern seaboard to the frontier. But now the heightened diversity in general taste—dress, music, food, entertainment—has impacted the world of religion, too. I'm sure it hasn't ended yet, but I wouldn't dare to suggest what the next change might be.

Thus today those leading worship may be in clerical robes (which themselves will vary from simple black to flamboyant colors and patterns) or business dress, open collar and slacks or torn-up blue jeans. Worship may begin with an intoned, "The Lord is in his holy temple; let all the earth keep silence before him," or, "Howdy, everybody! I hope you didn't run into too much trouble finding parking this morning. If you did, let me remind you that it was worse yesterday when you were tailgating at the stadium." And the music will range from Orthodox or Anglican chants to nineteenth-century gospel songs and twenty-first-century praise choruses. The accompaniment may be a pipe organ, a grand piano, a guitar, a jazz combo or a combination of several of the above. And of course in some bodies there is no instrumental accompaniment at all. Most people seem to have their preferences, and for some the preference is a fighting word.

And Where Are We Headed?

As several people (ranging from a Danish writer to Yogi Berra) have said, it's hard to make predictions, especially about the future. But I dare to suggest that in the matter of religious packaging—music, liturgy, costuming, preaching style—we have opened Pandora's box and things will never be the same. Where once people founded their religious community on the issue of doctrine, today probably more do so on what I'm calling the packaging. At the same time we shouldn't forget the tie between packaging and product, because in religion packaging and belief are related.

Let me be quick to say that packaging doesn't necessarily have much to do with the quality of the product. Certainly Dietrich Bonhoeffer's celebration of the sacrament in a Nazi prison was as authentic as the most magnificent service in a cathedral. Nevertheless, the packaging influences those who purchase the product and it affects the product itself. You see, we not only buy a product, we also buy the feeling it gives us. The Sunday school class I visited as a guest lecturer gave me a box of cookies. I ate the cookies with particular pleasure not only because of the quality of the cookies and the kindness they represented, but also the packaging, the very special box in which the cookies came. I saved the box. We save elements of our worship packaging too—not necessarily in a picture or a worship bulletin but in the ineffaceable venues of memory.

As I preach in various places across the nation, more often than not I preach in two or three different kinds of services on the same morning. In one I may preach in a clerical gown, in another in shirt-sleeves. (I tend to leave on my necktie because I like the ties my daughter gives me.) I preach the same message, but the packaging of delivery is different. In one service I am in the confines of a pulpit a dozen or twenty feet removed from the congregation, while in another I am on the same floor level with the hearer, and when I push aside the podium I am within two steps of those in the front row. This increased physical intimacy makes for a different kind of communication. It's the same message in both services, but I use different sentence structure, different speeds of delivery, different voice levels and certainly different gestures. On the whole I do this unconsciously, simply responding to the setting. The content is the same, but the packaging is different.

I feel as called to preach in one as in the other, and in my own way I am as much at home in one as in another, though I find the music in one more to my personal liking. By contrast, I ponder the Jews of old, for whom the city of worship was Jerusalem and the sacred experience was to occur in one place, the temple. When the temple was leveled to the ground by pagan invaders and many of the most loyal worshipers were carried off to Babylon, what happened to worship?

When the packaging is not simply remodeled but demolished, when the sacred place is trodden down by those who despise our faith, and when there is no historic, ordained place where you now live, how then do you worship?

The ancient biblical poet tells us how he felt. "By the rivers of Babylon—/ there we sat down and there we wept / when we remembered Zion." And when "tormentors" asked them to sing one of their songs of Zion, the poet cries, "How could we sing the LORD's song / in a foreign land?" (Ps 137:1, 4 NRSV). We're properly horrified when the poet concludes with a prayer that the children of his captors be violently destroyed, but I think this is the poet's way of saying that those who taunt him have no idea of the hurt they're causing, and the only way he can describe it is in language of pain they might be able to grasp.

But I dare to say that the psalmist was only talking about the packaging. Jerusalem was not God, nor was the temple. After all, when Solomon dedicated the temple he confessed, "If heaven, even the highest heaven, can't contain you, how can this temple that I've built contain you?" (1 Kings 8:27). Centuries later Jesus would tell the woman of Samaria that God is looking not for a place—packaging—but for people who will worship in spirit and in truth. I suspect that the psalmist in captivity would have been uneasy with such an idea, because for him the packaging was crucially important.

So What About the Packaging?

It's clear that packaging can attract and that it can also repel. In a culture where packaging is so important, from plastic surgery to skyscrapers and from book covers to the public persona of presidential candidates, it is also important to the church and the preacher. The packaging has more parts than we sometimes realize. When a group of my students met with Bishop Sundo Kim, the developer of one of the largest churches in the world, in Seoul, South Korea, one asked the secret of the church's growth. Bishop Kim's first two points were not surprising: good preaching and good music. But his third was different: good ushering. Ushering, including greeting, is part of the packaging. It matters especially to newcomers. In megachurches the directors in the parking area have the same ability to attract or discourage. That is, the worship experience begins with the parking lot, the greeters, the atmosphere of friendliness or the lack thereof.

I doubt that the packaging matters as much (if at all) for those who dare to become part of the house church movement in China, although some might say that the packaging—the intimacy and confined security of the small gathering in a sheltered place—is the essence of packaging. Basically, however, it's difficult to compare the growing churches of China, Africa and South America with the American scene. Both our secular culture and our religious culture are radically different from much of the rest of the world. American Protestants are accustomed to a choice, and many Roman Catholics now feel independent of the parish system. We're used to a business culture that caters to our wishes, so we expect our churches to be equally attentive.

Furthermore, our sense of institutional loyalty has diminished markedly in the past several decades. Where people once waited anxiously for membership in service clubs, lodges and golf clubs, many of these organizations now struggle to find enough members to maintain a viable program. Those of us who believe in the eternal mission of the church don't like to think that people look at their church the same way they look at their secular affiliations, but it's clear that many of them do. We hope to lead them to a higher loyalty, but first we have to get them started. And that involves, among other things, packaging.

But be properly cautious about any changes in packaging. If some new method (what people once called "cutting-edge") comes on the scene, don't believe that you're sure to succeed (whatever "success" means!) if you preach in the recommended style, employ the "new" pattern of liturgy and music, or establish a seeker-friendly architecture. One man's meat will drive another to being a vegan.

So What Shall We Do?

Let's begin with the obvious: whatever our packaging, we must do it well. We all agree that this is obvious but somehow a great many of us still miss the point. Seduced by the new, we launch out without proper preparation—especially if our church is currently in a doldrums. But a new style of preaching done poorly will have no more appeal than the old one. Maybe even less. I wonder how many churches have replaced dreary organ playing with an inept praise band only to discover that if they gained five people they also lost six. Mediocrity is exhausting in whatever form we deliver it. The secular media can afford to experiment, err and try again. It's more complicated for a church, not only because of finances but also because of the danger of hurting people in the process of change. No matter, we must start where we are, and whatever we do we must do well.

Further, we need to know our market. Since the tastes of our culture are so varied, we'd better have some idea of the people we hope to reach. Yes, everyone has a God-shaped void but it's a more reclusive void than it used to be, and we have to be more variety-sensitive if we hope to speak to it. When you see half-a-dozen churches opening in a new community you can be sure that several will drop by the wayside within a decade—and not because some lack earnestness or some pray with greater efficacy. In the language of the salesman in the classic musical *The Music Man,* "You've got to know the territory."

I don't want to confuse you, but having said that we need to know our market, let me also say that we should know the market well enough to sense the possibilities of the counterintuitive. Remember what varieties of people are among us. If "everyone" is looking for more spectacular electronics, someone might be wise to ignore electronics almost completely and concentrate on the human, the close-up, the familiar. Popular wisdom says that people are so accustomed to fast-moving sitcoms interrupted by multiple commercials that they won't put up with a sermon of more than eight or ten minutes. This seems logical, yet some congregations are building impressive attendance with forty-five minute, intensive biblical expositions. Harry Emerson Fosdick said famously in the 1920s that only the preacher thinks people come to church "desperately anxious to discover what happened to the Jebusites," yet some current preachers seem to have brought a form of the Jebusites back into the public domain.

What seems counterintuitive may indeed touch an unexpected void in many lives. A sensitive preacher, teacher or worship leader will look for something buried deep in the public opinion polls. Polls get answers that are shaped by the way the questions are asked. It's possible that we've been asking the wrong questions, so we've gotten only the obvious answers, or quite partial ones.

I worshiped recently in a congregation where a member of the church staff was giving a quite good children's sermon to a group of youngsters gathered around her at the front of the church. She was leading into her subject in a roundabout way. Suddenly a five- or six-year-old girl interrupted the speaker. "When are you going to talk about God?" Of course the congregation laughed. I wondered, however, how many adults might interrupt a sermon with the same question if they had a chance. It's possible that in postmodern attempts to be seeker-sensitive we have muffled our distinctive word. Some would call it counterintuitive to get so baldly religious. I submit that the counterintuitive may be our best-kept secret.

Public wisdom insists that the sermon must be relevant. I certainly wouldn't argue otherwise; the furthest thing from it. Yet many sermons work so hard at being relevant that they become trivial. Some statements and emphases that seem terribly significant for the moment are painfully insignificant six months later. It's dangerous to be captive to our times. When we try too hard to keep up with what is current we are in danger of becoming passé before the season ends.

We should also be wise enough to play to our strengths. What is it people look for when they come to church? Jesus raised the question for his own generation when he inquired into the phenomenon of John the Baptist. John had broken some obvious rules of preaching by making it physically difficult for people to come to him and by making nonnegotiable demands on those who sought his counsel. "What did you go out into the wilderness to see?" Jesus asked, then listed, half-playfully, all the things John the Baptist was not. He then reminded his audience of John's unique appeal as he repeated the question: "What did you go out to see? A prophet? Yes, I tell you, and more than a prophet" (Lk 7:24-26).

John the Baptist's strength was that he had a message from God. There were other intellectuals in Israel; the Sadducees had a good number. There were certainly some righteous men; the Pharisees would have counted perhaps six thousand. But John the Baptist was essentially unique. He had a word from God; he was a prophet in a land that hadn't seen a prophet in generations. John played to his strength.

Back to the matter of packaging. There are many ways to communicate a message in our twenty-first-century world. There is music, in

AUDIENCE PARTICIPATION WELCOME

Maybe preachers can learn a lesson from the comedy club. The comedians' sets in these smoky dark venues of typically crass humor are often punctuated by audience catcalls, interruptions and outright hostility—all depending on the amount of alcohol consumed by the guests. Sometimes the comedians will invite the audience to chime in. Whether planned or unplanned, there's something particularly engaging about the spontaneous input from the audience. It causes everyone to lean in just a little.

I'm not sure how that translates to a worship moment, but what if we preachers planned for moments in the message in which we invited the congregation to engage? This could help diffuse a distraction.

In my context that may mean something as simple as reading a text aloud in the midst of the message, asking people to say a brief phrase to the person next to them or conducting a quick poll by asking a question and inviting folks to raise their hands. Not only does this engage the congregation, it also creates freedom and space in a message for people to express themselves and develop an emotional attachment with the preacher. I have a hunch it prepares us and the congregation mentally for other kinds of distractions by creating a deeper bond between the preacher and the people.

Paul Clines, executive pastor, First United Methodist Church, Houston, Texas (Westchase Campus) varieties our ancestors could not have imagined. There is spectacle, with miracles of light and sound and combinations of the two that take our breath away, at least for a while. There is art; today we can transfer masterpieces of the centuries to a screen where all can enjoy them. And there's pageantry, a field where the church was once the primary authority. And visuals! When a preacher mentions Jerusalem, he or she can supplement the words with a picture on a screen. If the preacher refers to a movie, the AV team can cue up a film clip. When the preacher makes a point, he or she can underline and emphasize it by putting the words on screens to the right and left so that people can write down what was said.

Oral Communication

So what shall we say, then, about the preacher and teacher? Who are we?

We are the last of the oral communicators. Our world once knew Demosthenes and Socrates, Isaiah and Amos, Chrysostom and Augustine, Massillon and Donne, Calvin, Luther and Wesley, Beecher and Brooks, Billy Sunday, Billy Graham and Martin Luther King Jr. Does oral communication still appeal today? There was a time when people paid admission to hear a lecture by Charles Dickens or Ralph Waldo Emerson, or more recently by William Lyon Phelps or Dale Carnegie. Not many if any could charge admission today and make a living. Once upon a time people gathered at a whistle stop by the hundreds or the thousands to catch a glimpse of presidential candidates and to hear a few words from the back railing of a railroad club car, but today who cares about personal oral communication?

When the apostle declared the way of salvation, he insisted that "faith comes from listening" and "how can they hear without a preacher?" (Rom 10:17, 14). Do we need to bring the apostle up to date? Perhaps "faith comes by watching, and how can they watch without a drama or a movie?" Or "faith comes by attention-demanding sensations, and how can there be such without the best sound effects and strobe lights?"

I'm not disparaging the use of twenty-first-century media, but I do want us to remember that there is something special—indeed irreplaceable—about the human voice speaking intelligible words. I am happy to see that kind of communication transmitted by radio and television (I have used such media through my own lifetime of preaching). Nevertheless, I believe there is something uniquely powerful in a human being who is physically present with other humans, using voice, words, eyes, gestures and soul. I'm sure we should use every means possible to convey the eternal message, from printed page to iPhone and Twitter. But in the end I don't believe that anything can replace the intimacy and insistency of a human being talking with other human beings—and talking with them so effectively that the speaker in turn hears what the listeners are saying so that the message has an immediacy no other medium can fully duplicate.

That is: We must not give up the ancient power of the prophet, the pastor, the evangelist. But we must hone our skills to do business with an Age of Distraction.

What Packaging Works Best?

If packaging is important—and it is, and always has been—what packaging is best for this Age of Distraction? More particularly, when the secular culture has become so expert in packaging and has such vast resources to exercise its power, how can preaching and worship compete? Perhaps some would ask if we should even try. But of course that isn't an option, because we're in the competition even if we don't like the word. People are constantly choosing where they will invest their attention and their souls, and it is our calling to get a fair hearing for Christ and faith.

I won't say much about music or about worship in general, since the burden of this book is preaching. But overall I am uneasy with the passion for the new that currently influences both the Protestant and Catholic world and the general faddishness that dominates so much of the evangelical world in particular. At the least I would recommend the counsel Alexander Pope gave some four hundred years ago: "Be not the first by whom the new are tried, / nor yet the last to lay the old aside."[2] We should always be learning, but an early rule of learning is to be discriminating. That something is new does not mean it is good or effective; primarily, it means that it is still being tested. The Food and Drug Administration insists on proper testing before allowing a new drug on the market lest health or lives be lost. In the church we should test ideas thoroughly before we institute something that may hurt more than bless.

We also do well to respect the past. There are reasons why some things endure while others are forgotten before the paint is fully dry. It is almost by definition that we Christians are people of the book and of tradition. This means we have a foot in the past and that we see the present and the future through the heritage of that past.

And by all means we should never confuse our personal taste with God's taste. We have a right to prefer a particular melody, style, instrument or ritual, but so do those whose taste is different from our own. Our human limitations don't limit God. I think fondly of a man who often sat beside me at a weekly men's prayer breakfast. He sang on only one note but with a lovely earnestness. When I got into a proper spirit, I was blessed by his singing.

Above all, in the packaging of worship, including preaching, we should make certain that we do not lose the product in the packaging.

We should remind ourselves constantly that the worship our Lord desires is that which is marked by spirit and truth (Jn 4:23-24).

As for preaching, many of our choices have to do with our own style and with the nature of our denominational heritage and the tastes of our people. What a congregation enjoys in a guest speaker or in a television personality may not be what they want in their own pastor or teacher. It's something like what people say of a certain city or area: a nice place to visit but I wouldn't want to live there.

What style of preaching is best? Line-by-line exposition? A series of points and illustrations that prove a point? Narrative? Visuals and object lessons? I confess readily that I like some better than others and that I like some only by exercising more effort. But in any event, I like to hear a preacher who does it well. Several years ago I visited a church known over several generations for its outstanding expository preaching. It was full both Sunday morning and evening, inconvenient parking notwithstanding. Several of my former students employ visuals in every sermon, and they do it effectively. A great deal depends on the makeup of the congregation, what they are accustomed to, and the preacher's own skill in the method used. If you are concerned about the level of your congregation's attentiveness or response, it would be good to give another preaching style a chance. You may have skills of which you have been unaware.

I think it is important, in this Age of Distraction, to be careful that our packaging doesn't add to the distraction. We are told that most people—especially the youth and young adults—are accustomed to multitasking. True, perhaps, to a point. Yet there are times when full attention is demanded. When two people in love are having dinner in a favorite setting, they don't want multitasking or divided attention. If the eyes of the other are exploring other diners or wandering to a television screen, the wonder of the evening is broken.

The greater the issue before us, the more important the focus of attention. If we believe that the gospel is a life-and-death matter, we will want to keep distractions to a minimum. Do we take five minutes to tell a two-minute story? If so, we're building a distraction of boredom into the story, and we may never regain full attention. Does the order of worship include some fill-in-the-blank sermon helps? If so, chances are that after filling in the present blank the listener's mind will turn off until the next step in the little game of sermon-prepping. Do we have some gesture that's irritating or some mannerism that offends? We might do well to invest some money with a coach who knows both content and delivery and put ourselves through the pain of examination.

Do visual aids (the pictures flashed on a screen or the outline words) aid comprehension or do they distract? The answer depends partly on the nature of the sermon. The outline notes may help a sermon that is more of an informational lecture. Not so with a sermon that aims for total, accumulative impact rather than specific points of development. The scene from the Sea of Galilee may be so captivating that the listener stays at Galilee while the speaker is moving on to eternity. It's a judgment call.

Much is said about our ability to entertain several ideas and impressions at the same time. Consider this, however. When television is reporting news, it may have a line or two at the bottom of the screen offering other data—a breaking headline or stock market figures, for instance; the sports station carries one or two lines of scores under the action from the playing field. Rarely, however, is there such a bottom line during a commercial. Why not? Because those who are paying for the time want to be sure they have as much of our attention as possible. Preachers should be very sure they are not competing with themselves by placing auxiliary material on a screen or in the bulletin. Be sure, that is, that the point of the sermon is not killed by your own friendly fire.

Packaging is important. It always has been, and our knowledge of human psychology has made it still more so. The preacher and teacher want to be sure that the packaging is attractive but, more than that, that it is true to its contents. In a world of distractions, the sermon and worship packaging must be servant to the truth it carries.

MODELS OF PREACHING

While the word "attract" often has an alluring sense to it, the Latin source for our English word "distract" carries with it a more visceral connotation: literally, distraction means "to drag away." It doesn't matter if we're preachers or we're being preached to. We've all been dragged away. It's a problem older than Scripture itself. Whether we're in the garden with Adam and Eve or there with Jesus' disciples on the night of his betrayal, we are under constant threat of distraction. Not even David, Israel's greatest king, was immune from it. In 2 Samuel 11:1, we discover that something is rotten in the state of Denmark—or, in this case, Jerusalem. Samuel begins the chapter by telegraphing: "In the spring, at the time when kings go off to war . . . " (NIV). While responsible kings were out with their armies, Israel's king was somewhere else entirely. Samuel ends verse one with this abrupt observation: "But David remained in Jerusalem." Israel's king was distracted, and before long many others were dragged into the mess he created.

More than twenty years ago, Comedy Central used to air a program called *Short Attention Span Theater*. Those of us who preach regularly can identify with the challenge of communicating to "short attention span congregations." By the same token, preachers are not immune either. Like filings drawn to a magnet, all of us can be dragged away by our own powerful distractions. Fortunately, preachers have many models at their disposal to assist them with this challenge. Here are just a few examples:

In recent decades, series preaching has grown in popularity in many places. With this model, preachers build from one sermon to the next by focusing a series around one biblical book or theme over a span of weeks. With this model, preachers and their congregations can benefit from greater weekly continuity as well as opportunities to drill down more deeply, exploring lessons across an entire series and hopefully resulting in greater application and implication. Given today's penchant for instant gratification, however, preachers should likely resist the urge to preach long sermon series today, opting for shorter-length series instead.

Another preaching model growing in popularity is the dialogical sermon, which includes opportunities for congregational members to explore the biblical text during the sermon itself. Opportunities are given by the preacher for questions and responses by the laity, much in the same way that a spirited classroom discussion takes place. By inviting congregational exploration of the sermon text, the dialogical sermon offers opportunities for meaningful congregational engagement.

A classic preaching method used in many sermons could be called the "call and response" or "fill in the blank" delivery method. This model of verbal delivery invites the congregation to respond to the preacher's query for a specific word or phrase within the sermon itself. Preachers who are adept at this method preach in ways that call for laypeople to provide the missing words, not on a printed outline but verbally in response to the preacher. For instance, the call-and-response preacher might say something like, "The apostle Paul tells us that we're saved by grace through what?" The congregation responds verbally with the word "faith." This preaching method has historical support in some types of congregations more than others, but the practice itself can engage worshipers who might otherwise be in danger of being dragged off by distractions.

Jay Richard Akkerman, professor of pastoral theology, Northwest Nazarene University, Nampa, Idaho

THE INSISTENT POWER
OF SERMON CONTENT

A preacher in the first quarter of this twenty-first century can feel kinship with an anonymous servant of the prophet Elisha. The king of Aram had heard that Elisha was somehow privy to his military plans and then passing the information to Israel's king, thus thwarting Aram's attacks. He decided to get rid of Elisha. So it was that Elisha's servant awakened one morning to see "an army with horses and chariots surrounding the city." In panic he appealed to Elisha. "Oh, no! Master, what will we do?" Elisha answered with what must have been exasperating calm. "Don't be afraid, because there are more of us than there are of them." With that, Elisha prayed that his servant's eyes be opened—and with the prayer, the servant "saw that the mountain was full of horses and fiery chariots surrounding Elisha" (2 Kings 6:15-17).

I understand the distress of Elisha's servant, because we preachers have a similar problem. We hear daily about Aram's twenty-first-century army with its horses and chariots; they surround the holy encampment of the church on every side. Secularism and materialism, the formidable graven images of our day, increase daily in numbers and in their appeal. The overall moral culture of our society seems more corrupting year after year. In an analysis of language usage since 1960, *New York Times* columnist David Brooks concludes, "Over the past half century, society has become more individualistic. As it has become more individualistic, it has also become less morally aware."[1] The words that dominate our speech are an impressive barometer of our soul state. The challenge of the distracted soul becomes more daunting year after year.

With what armaments can the preacher respond? We might answer bravely, "The sword of the Spirit, which is the Word of the Lord." But a quaver in the voice indicates that many in our army fear that ours is a rusted sword. Privately, many of us wish we had war materiel more appropriate to the kinds of battles that engage us in these postmodern times. I daresay that some preaching suggests we are better acquainted with the style and armaments of our culture than with the traditional armory of the kingdom. Even among those who declare their loyalty to the Scriptures there is a tacit confession of defeat in that the old verities—if mentioned—are not proclaimed with the passion of another day.

The Outlook for Preaching

As for preaching itself, some predict that the outlook is dreary. The preacher and teacher realize that faith comes by hearing, as the apostle declared, and specifically that it is by hearing the Word of the Lord. And we know that Paul spoke a relentless rhetorical question: "And how can they hear without a preacher?" (Rom 10:14). But what if fewer and fewer are listening to the preacher? What if the preacher's voice is nearly drowned out by the din and dynamite of competing voices? What if the preacher's voice is made dull by the distractions of a kind of intellectual and spiritual tinnitus?

Such a problem is not new. "Preaching has become a by-word for a long and dull conversation of any kind, and whoever wishes to imply, in any piece of writing, the absence of everything agreeable and inviting, calls it a sermon."[2] It was a clergyman who said that, Sydney Smith (1771–1845). Jonathan Swift, also a clergyman but better known as the author of *Gulliver's Travels*, obviously doubted the value of sermons: "The preaching of divines helps to preserve well-inclined men in the course of virtue, but seldom, or never, reclaims the vicious."[3] Ralph Waldo Emerson wrote in one of his most famous essays, "I like the silent church before the service begins better than any preaching."[4] Emerson set out to be a preacher but gained his fame as an essayist and later as a lecturer—in both of which he seemed often to sound like a preacher, but without a gospel. And if this is the sort of thing that preachers and former preachers say about the profession, one wonders what the atheist says, or the pagan. Perhaps they offer the most damning commentary by not bothering to attack preaching as such.

I repeat, preaching has always had a hard time of it. If you want to know how magnificent and timeless sermons can be and how trying it may be to preach them, just follow the Hebrew prophets from Elijah to Zechariah. And it gets no easier in the New Testament. The apostle Paul is as good an authority on preaching as we're likely to find; he described it as "the foolishness of preaching." He divided the world's audience into two parts, Jews and Gentiles, then summed up the reception gospel preaching received as "a scandal to Jews and foolishness to Gentiles" (1 Cor 1:23).

Having said that, Paul nevertheless continued preaching. Indeed, he preached at a fearful price, knowing that wherever he went there would be not only times of indifference, controversy, scorn and outright rejection, but also of physical persecution, imprisonment and, possibly, death. He was sure of some things that made all of these impediments and threats quite meaningless. For one, because although at the human side the message was dismissed as scandal and foolishness, it proved when accepted to be "God's power and God's wisdom." And from the divine side, "God was pleased to save those who believe through the foolishness of preaching" (1 Cor 1:21). If preaching makes an eternal difference to those who choose to hear it, and if God acts in support of preaching, it can't be as helpless and hopeless as we sometimes fear.

The first-century world saw the preaching of the cross as foolishness, but ultimately this foolishness of God proves wise. From what I can see, this dichotomy of the divine and human definitions of wisdom and foolishness has never changed. Sometimes the difference is more vigorously marked than at others, but the difference remains. Sometimes, at least on the surface, the response to preaching changes. But century after century preaching has to make its way against odds. This is partly because we humans never like to be told how we should live; since we left Eden it has been part of our DNA to resent being told we are wrong and that we need to change. And no doubt another part of the problem has been the quality of preaching. In truth, it is strange that God would entrust such a priceless product to be delivered by such unlikely vessels as human sermons. But that's the way it is, and it's up to us preachers and teachers to do the best we can with the assignment we've received. We may be vessels of clay, but we're vessels that God has shaped and chosen.

I have bet most of my life on preaching, and my mind hasn't changed. Yes, I do have some caveats. I tell my preaching students that they have no greater enemy than the poor preacher, because poor preaching makes poor listeners, and poor listeners in turn make for still more poor (or discouraged) preachers. Poor preaching lowers the expectations of the people who come, and it drives out those individuals who hunger for something better. Poor preaching discredits the product it represents. It's dreadful to think of anything that makes the cross of Christ commonplace or that reduces the grace of God to a byword.

By poor preaching I mean preaching that is insincere or that is carelessly prepared (which, in truth, is another expression of insincerity). By poor preaching I mean preaching that is without a gospel—that is, without the good news of Christ that brings salvation. By poor preaching I mean preaching that is short on love for God and for the human race. By poor preaching I mean preaching that is not doctrinally sound. By poor preaching I mean preaching that is not winsome and persuasive. By poor preaching I mean preaching that does not bring salvation to sinners and growth in Christ to believers.

The length of sermons is not in itself a major issue. I wish that all of us preachers, however, would remember a basic rule: what matters is not how long we preach but how long the hearer listens, not how much we say but how much people comprehend and apply to their lives. On the whole, sermons are shorter than they were fifty years ago. This isn't necessarily bad, if the time is used well. It's probably true that television, with its many commercial breaks and its constant scene shifting, has affected our ability to concentrate.

Personally, I'm impressed that nearly three centuries ago one of the greatest pulpit orators of history, George Whitefield, said, "To preach more than half an hour, a man should be an angel and have angels for hearers."[2] Whitefield did most of his fabled preaching in open fields, without amplification, to crowds where many if not most were standing. He had to speak above the rustling of a crowd. Believe me, such a crowd will need to be spellbound, because even if the average person is only shifting from one foot to the other or adjusting the coat jacket, if you multiply the sound by several thousand persons it will begin to drown out the speaker. The greatest actors of the period envied Whitefield his oratorical skills. But greater still was his common sense: don't put the endurance of your audience to a test, and don't be presumptuous about your own histrionic abilities.

The proper length depends on the speaker, the listener and, yes, the touch of the Holy Spirit. Some have learned to condense their message into ten minutes while others dare to speak for forty-five. Some who speak forty-five minutes for their own congregation find that they had better stop at twenty to twenty-five minutes when the hearers are un-accustomed to their style. Sometimes there is an attentiveness in the audience that comes with an electricity in the air, something we sense to be a special evidence of the presence of God. But the preacher who presumes upon such a moving as an indication that he or she can speak longer may find that the lights go out in a hurry when the wonder is gone. Some brain research indicates that the first twenty minutes of anything (sermon, meeting, class) is the most optimal time for attention and learning; after that, it goes down precipitously. We preachers would do well not to put our sermons to the test.

Content: Scripture

My primary concern is the matter of content. After the oratorical flourishes are gone and the personality of the speaker is only a memory, it is the content that matters. So what did the apostle have in mind when he spoke of God's foolishness, a foolishness that would get to both Jew and Gentile, both the patently religious and the proudly pagan?

A MEMORABLE DISTRACTION

When I began preaching more than sixty years ago, the greatest distractions when I stood in the pulpit were the crying babies in my congregation. Now the babies are gone, thanks to modern nurseries. But in their place have come the ubiquitous cell phones with their great variety of musical rings and the urgency everybody feels to answer them, even in the most public and inconvenient moments.

The biggest distraction I ever had to preach around (there was no preaching through it) was the Sunday that eighty-year-old Claggett Jones rose from his pew, staggered into the center aisle of the church, and collapsed from a heart attack. There were a lot of doctors present, and soon so many had gathered around Claggett that someone said, "Get back! Give the poor man some air!"

By the time a stretcher had been produced and Claggett was being carried up the aisle to the rear of the church, he had recovered enough to reach in his pocket and hold aloft his pledge card, as it was Pledge Sunday. I had been preaching a sermon about stewardship, but Claggett's gesture trumped everything I had been trying to say, and that year we had the best pledge drive anybody in the church could remember!

John Killinger, author of *101 Tips for New Ministers*

Start with this: that to be human is to have a capacity for God—indeed, an insistent capacity. Neural scientists are venturing that perhaps there is something in the human brain that instinctively reaches out to God. We are so created that we look for something or someone beyond ourselves. When Augustine said of God, "You have made us for yourself, and our heart is restless until it rests in you," he may have been as much a scientist as a theologian. What science now approaches tentatively (which is of course the proper scientific posture) the poet has always declared. Francis Thompson, the nineteenth-century British poet, called it "The Hound of Heaven"—those "strong Feet that followed, followed after," even as "I fled Him, down the arches of the years;" and "down the labyrinthine ways / Of my own mind; and in the mist of tears." I submit that those "strong Feet" have been on our human trail since in a long-ago Eden God called, "Where are you?" (Gen 3:9).

Let me go a step further. When, as the inspired historian-poet-philosopher who gave us Genesis tells us, God "formed the human from the topsoil of the fertile land and blew life's breath into his nostrils" (Gen 2:7), we humans got enough of God that we will never be satisfied except in the fuller measure that we let God into our lives. Therefore, the preacher has a head start on every person who settles into a pew, a theater seat or a folding chair to hear him or her. However dull of interest the listener may appear to be, and however distracted by the uncounted voices that clamor for attention, the preacher's claim was there first. The breath came from God. The soul bears the branding of eternity, no matter how transient its pursuits, no matter how trivial its ambitions.

Zedekiah, king of Judah, was not a saint; he was not even an honorable king. He paid no attention to "the LORD's words spoken by the prophet Jeremiah" (Jer 37:2). Nevertheless, there came a time when

King Zedekiah sent for Jeremiah "and questioned [him] secretly in the palace: 'Is there a word from the LORD?'" (Jer 37:17). Zedekiah wasn't a very desirable congregant. His primary motivation was self-preservation, and a tough-minded prophet must have felt that Zedekiah was a superstitious man who might have been more satisfied with a fortuneteller than with a prophet. Nevertheless, Zedekiah was seeking "a word from the Lord." Don't waste time discrediting the suppliant's credentials; just answer the request and see where the conversation goes from there.

The basic scenario remains the same today. Only the name and office of Zedekiah have changed. It seems that each time there's a great natural disaster—or at a more personal level, a tragic automobile accident or house fire—the television reporter closes the interview, "The family [or the bereaved] is in our thoughts and prayers."

The preacher, toughened by life in a secular society, sometimes christens such remarks as "a meaningless mantra." A mantra it may be, and as such it may be something the newsperson will forget in the midst of tomorrow's sports and political headlines and entertainment gossip. So it is too with much of the television or Internet audience. But mantras are never meaningless. Such formulaic sayings exist and survive because we humans need them. They are vital to our emotional existence, because they carry a seed of truth. Yes, and even when the truth is twisted and cheapened by poor understanding. The preacher and teacher must never forget that human hunger is on our side, and we dare not grow cynical because of its ebb and flow. God has a stake in the human soul that is prior to all its other inclinations.

For this reason I speak of the insistent power of our message. Consider by contrast Dietrich Bonhoeffer's experience when he came to America in the 1930s. Bonhoeffer visited a wide variety of New York churches, seeking to become acquainted with America in general and its religious life in particular. He was shocked by what he found. "The sermon has been reduced to parenthetical church remarks, about newspaper events." They preach, he wrote to his friends and family in Germany, "about virtually everything; only one thing is not addressed, or is addressed so rarely that I have as yet been unable to hear it, namely, the gospel of Jesus Christ, the cross, sin and forgiveness, death and life."[3]

That is, the preaching was trivial and superficial. The church is entrusted with the one indispensable message, the only ultimate human necessity. How ironical, then, if we neglect this word and in its place offer what can be found anywhere.

Each new survey tells us that we live in a biblically illiterate culture. We hear that great numbers of people can name only four or five of the ten commandments and even fewer of the twelve apostles. This news is no longer shocking, and perhaps that's what should concern us most. A veteran salesman in a secular field would see such a situation as evidence of a market wide open for his product.

It is time for the preacher to see how fortunate he or she is in having a message that is indispensable to the human race, one that in a sense has been neglected for a generation or more. Meanwhile, on the secular side, the market is surfeited. Pity, if you will, those who seek a spectacle more spectacular than last season's spectacle. Worry for those who have to develop the half-time entertainment for the next Super Bowl, or the multimillion-dollar commercials to fill the time-out moments. Ancient Rome had to find new ways to pit animals against humans in the coliseum, because ordinary blood and death had become boring. I expect that some entertainment mogul is wondering if there isn't a fifth dimension of reality or the surreal that can bring the jaded to the box office.

Envy the preacher, because the preacher has the Bible. The Bible is old enough to have the authority of time, but for many it is now unfamiliar enough to be new. Perhaps even a novelty! The preacher must take the Bible at its word. The Reverend Fleming Rutledge reminds us that "if the Scripture has one controlling presupposition from beginning to end, it is the power of the Word of God. We can't have the Bible without that affirmation. 'God *said*, "Let there be light," *and there was light.*'" We need not be apologetic about this, nor shrill. It is the ground on which we stand. As Ms. Rutledge puts it, "A Bible construed without the Word as power is not the Bible at all."[4]

> Kierkegaard believed that our worship itself is a distraction from the presence of God, and that this situation will not be corrected until we realize that we are on stage, not in the audience, acting out our faith before Almighty God, who is the audience.
>
> *John Killinger*

It was not a Christian but a Jew, and not a theologian but a novelist (and a Nobel Prize-winning novelist at that) who compared the insights of Genesis with Homer's *Iliad* and *Odyssey* and with contemporary science. "There is little comfort," the late Isaac Bashevis Singer wrote, "in the science of today and in its cosmology. It has filled the universe with idols we can never love or even respect." By contrast, Singer continued, "No matter how the human brain might grow, it will always come back to the idea that God has created heaven and earth, man and animals, with a will and a plan, and that, despite all the evil life undergoes, there is a purpose in Creation and eternal wisdom."[5] It is a privilege to preach from such a book!

Content: Doctrine

We have doctrine to proclaim, and we get to proclaim it in a culture that is morally and intellectually adrift. In a culture of the transient gods that now inhabit the "spirituality" section of our favorite bookstores, we can present the God Isaiah met after King Uzziah died. For a generation that professes to love Jesus but wants nothing to do with the church or Christians, we can introduce one who was conceived by the Holy Spirit, born of the Virgin Mary, who descended into hell and now sits at the right hand of God. Such a Jesus takes our breath away, even while he invites us to bring our burdens to him. And it is very good to come to know him, because one day he will judge the quick and the dead. This world that spends billions annually to preserve its bodies by regimens of exercise and dieting and to improve its lines by plastic surgery, hear the good news: our bodies are of such worth that we believe they will someday be resurrected. How can a preacher resist declaring such doctrine?

Can doctrine get a hearing in our time? The books in the New Age section of a bookstore indicate that it can. Perhaps you hadn't thought of those books as doctrine, but primarily this is what they offer. To whatever measure they succeed, it is because of their ability to make their teachings interesting and relevant to the average person—the religious or semireligious seeker. Dr. Timothy Keller has demonstrated that doctrinal preaching can appeal to a sociological group that many would have thought unreachable: young urban professionals in New York City. In a period of twenty years he has built a congregation with a weekly attendance of five thousand on three campuses in a city that could be described as hostile to God, or at least terminally indifferent. But his preaching and his bestselling books have emphasized basic Christian doctrine: books like *The Reason for God*, *The Prodigal God* and *Counterfeit Gods*.

I have found that people in my own denomination only rarely know their specific doctrinal heritage. In this postmodern day where "whatever one believes is okay for them," people more than ever need a belief system. Doctrine can be exciting by way of a series of sermons on the Apostles' Creed or sermons related to specific days on the church calendar. Advent and Christmastime appeal to childhood sentiment; we can get inside the story and unfold doctrines like the incarnation and salvation. I submit that there's enough doctrine in the Charles Wesley carol "Hark! the Herald Angels Sing" to save any soul, if only listeners really hear it.

Many megachurches have served their constituencies by preaching to their felt needs. I honor this, and I surely praise any instance where it is done well. I have chosen rather to emphasize preaching with its base in the Scriptures and in Christian doctrine because of my deep conviction that eventually these matters must come forward. They are indispensable. We have forgotten their potential or have been slow to appreciate it. Perhaps we can learn from a great journalist of another day, G. K. Chesterton (*Orthodoxy*), a premier scholar and storyteller, C. S. Lewis (*Mere Christianity*), or a master of mystery stories, Dorothy Sayers (*Creed or Chaos?*), that doctrine and Scripture are exciting.

Some of us may have decided that the twenty-first-century person has no interest in Scripture and even less in doctrine. To counter this, we would do well to read those preachers and novelists and poets who have told the story with enchantment and then seek out the enchantment that lies in our own person. There is insistent power and authority in the Scriptures and the doctrines of the faith that have come from those Scriptures. It's an Age of Distraction, yes. But the basic need exists, as it always will, and we preachers are gifted with riveting material to speak to our times, distraction notwithstanding.

10

THE PREACHER'S
SECRET RESOURCES

I remember a phrase from my Iowa childhood. It reflects a simple world, one where we knew little or nothing about balanced diets or about plates with several colors of fruits and vegetables that promised both beauty and nutrition. We didn't worry about culinary variety or imagination. The phrase said it all: "It's easy to feed a hungry man."

The same truism applies to pulpit diet. Hungry souls make an ordinary preacher look like a pulpit genius. I can't help feeling that there are as many hungry souls in the world as ever. Unfortunately, most of them don't know they're hungry because most of them are on a heavy diet of fast food. And even among those who know they're hungry, few can imagine that they're hungry to hear a sermon. Yes, they would enjoy some music, especially if delivered by a symphonic chorale or a winsome country and western star (depending on their tastes). And yes, drama appeals to them, as found in a little theater just off Broadway or on television or at the movies. But a sermon? Who could be that hungry?

I know. I've been preaching sermons for longer than you would believe, and I've listened to them for even longer than that. I've heard boring sermons and inspiring ones, sermons that I still remember half a century later and some that I forgot before the benediction. I've heard some of the most notable preachers of the twentieth century, beginning with Billy Sunday, and a little later Harry Emerson Fosdick, Ralph W. Sockman and George Buttrick. It's too early to say who are most notable in this twenty-first century. You, the reader, may prove to be one of this century's notables. But though I've heard thousands of sermons and preached thousands, I still try to hear more, and I still pull for the preacher from wherever I sit.

I pull especially hard for today's preachers because I feel that they are preaching in uniquely challenging times. The human need is as great as ever, but in many people this need is well hidden. In the face of these challenges, it's time that we looked at our resources. Some of these resources may seem like old stuff to you; if so, I'm suggesting that you give them another look—they may have changed, or you may have.

Ministering to the Overfed

But first, consider a key problem the preacher faces. We minister to the overfed. Overfed is not the same thing, of course, as well-nourished. As surely as we can be physically obese while being seriously undernourished, we can suffer from mental and spiritual obesity while starving for real spiritual and intellectual nourishment.[1] Unfortunately we have no spiritual body mass index system to measure our condition.

When Moses told the Israelite slaves that he would lead them to freedom, they rejected him. "But they didn't listen to Moses," Exodus reports, "because of their complete exhaustion and their hard labor" (Ex 6:9). What do exhaustion and hard labor have to do with our twenty-first-century lives? Well, have you noticed how many frazzled and preoccupied people you run into? Twenty-first-century traffic, which vast numbers of people face daily, doesn't offer the contemplative feeling of a meandering country road. As for communication, it has become a traffic jam of its own. Letter writers in the past hoped for an answer in several days or a week; today a student who emails me in the morning might send a follow-up at noon, wondering if I'm not well because he hasn't yet heard from me. Organized social media at first seemed like a nice way to keep up with our friends. Now we find that if we affiliate with one or more of these bodies, they own us; we feel compelled to keep up. Some of the compelling is from old-fashioned curiosity, and some of it from the worthy feeling that we should respond to the information we've received. Thus the activity that we thought would be fun becomes demanding even to the point of exhaustion. Douglas Rushkoff, author of *Present Shock*, is not as concerned with what technology might be doing to people as he is with "what people are choosing to do to one another through technology."[2]

Hard labor? A substantial number of families not only have two members in the employed workforce, but one of those individuals also has two or more jobs—some because they can't provide life's necessities without two jobs, others because they're accustomed to a certain standard of living and find it difficult to settle back to more modest circumstances. We commonly think of America as the greatest place on earth; sociologists observe that this conviction has turned in on us. If this is the best there is—this world of two or three jobs, living from one paycheck to another, gaining some luxuries but less time to enjoy them—if this is the best there is, there's no winning the ball game! These are the overfed who are dying of spiritual malnourishment. The problem is not only the poor nourishment of what they're eating, but also the problem of what's eating them.

We preachers need to see this pain and gain the Christ-compassion to enter into the pain of the people to whom we minister. I remember a pastoral evening when I called on newcomers to the community who had visited our church once or twice. The man quoted Henry David Thoreau to describe what he and his wife were experiencing: "The mass of men live lives of quiet desperation." I think of him still as I observe the world around me and listen to its voices. Quiet desperation is a long way from Jesus' offer of a more abundant life.

I'm thinking too of our emotional saturation point. Let's call it ennui, that feeling of weariness and discontent resulting from satiety or lack of interest. The key word in that definition is *satiety*, which is the condition of being satisfied to the point of boredom. Is there a limit to our sensory equipment so that having passed the limit we drop into an abyss of boredom? I suspect that sensation feeds on itself until at last satisfaction is lost in boredom. In a world of distractions, ennui may be the coming plague.

All of which says that we humans must become experts in making choices. Obviously, choice-making isn't a new human skill; it has been our mark of distinction for as long as we know. But now the choice-making issue has become increasingly demanding simply by multiplying its faces and thus its omnipresence. Only rarely do these choices seem recognizably significant, but of course choice-making is a cumulative process. Choice A leads to choice B—perhaps both of them innocent in themselves—and eventually to a situation where we are clearly compelled to choose between good and evil. But by that time our prior choices may make us unconsciously prejudiced toward a less moral way, or even drawn to it.

This is where the preacher comes in, because by definition the preacher ought to be the resident expert in discerning the difference between good and evil. This process of distinction begins with knowing the difference between the good and the not so good. Those things that are not so good eventually prove themselves to be evil, because in time they crowd out the good. This is the issue in our use of time. We cannot say it clearly and persuasively enough. When one is dealing with a limited resource—and time is the most rigidly limited of all our resources—one has to realize that ultimately the choice is between good and evil. If the best is crowded out by the better and the better by the good, eventually all that is left is a dull average. That dull average is below the purposes of God. I dare to believe that God created us humans to rise above such a level. Our basic Christian goal must always be the fullness of the image of our Lord Jesus Christ. Anything that leads us in the opposite direction leads us away from God.

Preaching has never been for the faint of heart. If we believe in God and in eternity, and if we have proper regard for our fellow human creatures, preaching is the most demanding of callings. We're performing soul surgery each time we pursue our calling. Now the stress level is still higher because of the complexity of choices in our Age of Distraction and because it's so difficult for us to understand that even minor choices—especially where time is involved—become fateful choices.

The Preacher Cares

From a secular point of view, it seems that the social networking of the Internet came just in time to save us from the anonymity of television. It's not that television and radio weren't trying. The bright minds in those systems of communication know that they must make the listener or viewer feel singularly important. Herein lies the

MEETING THE NEED FOR DISTRACTION

The question we need to ask ourselves is the degree to which distraction is a choice. Certainly there are times when I am the unwitting victim of distraction. I am earnestly trying to focus and concentrate, but something internal or external comes along to draw my attention away.

At other times, however, I must confess that I am a volunteer for distraction. Indeed, I seek it. Many times in many ways, we avoid thinking about something that is painful, challenging, worrisome, confusing or sad by choosing instead to distract ourselves with something else. It may be that a fair amount of our entertainment functions in this way for us: it is deliberate, voluntary distraction.

For as long as we don't know what action to take, we frequently take no action. And for as long as we don't know what emotion we're feeling or how to deal with it, we try not to feel it. We seek distractions as detours that we think will take us around the difficult thing or situation about which we don't know what to do or how to feel. If we are fortunate, our voluntary distractions do not cause too much damage before we come to Charles Wesley's realization: "Other refuge have I none; hangs my helpless soul on Thee."

Perhaps it is at this level that the preacher does not need to be entirely antagonistic to the human need for distraction. Indeed, perhaps we can help to meet that need. After all, folks arrive in our pews every Sunday with a lot on their minds and hearts, and some part of them may be eager to think about something else.

The poignant invitation of Edmund Sears's familiar Christmas carol comes to mind. In "It Came Upon a Midnight Clear" he calls out to those who are bowed under life's crushing load, who toil and climb "with painful steps and slow." He invites them to "rest beside the weary road, and hear the angels sing!" Perhaps the weary souls in need of distraction should experience such a lovely relief and ministering evangel when they come into our churches.

David J. Kalas, senior pastor, First United Methodist Church, Green Bay, Wisconsin

peculiar appeal of radio call-in shows, where devotees of sports and politics can talk with their guru or get the experience secondhand as they hear someone else do so. Television has its deep friendships on the home shopping stations. Those who camp there feel that the person on the screen is their friend, someone who really wants them to look better, feel better and enjoy life more. Many of us know individuals who buy unneeded items from such television programs primarily because they think the spokesperson cares about them.

The social media of the Internet have taken this matter to a whole new level. Through its magic we not only can keep up with the welfare of an ever-widening circle of "friends," we can also know what an entertainer had for breakfast or how a professional athlete happens at this moment to feel about his coach or manager. Even the pope is now a Twitter companion.

I don't know how much more this system of faux friendship and intimacy will grow; at this moment the market seems insatiable. I do know, however, that the Internet and the cell phone tell us how much we humans want to know that somebody cares about us.

No one is in a better position to fill that need than the pastor-preacher. Indeed, this is the name of our calling. We are pastors; we watch over our sheep. And if our heart is as God ordained it to be, we see all individuals as potentially part of our fold—not necessarily in the sense of their uniting formally with our religious body, but in the sense that we are ready to care about them and if possible to minister to them.

In my years as a pastor I tried to be a good preacher, and there are those who thought I succeeded. But so often when I meet persons from thirty or forty years ago, they recite their memory of a hospital visit, or my coming to their home in their time of trouble, or my sending them a card when I was on vacation. The only genius in this is the genius of caring, of giving attention to someone.

In the small-town world of my first parish, strolling down Main Street on Friday evening meant chatting with members and constituents. It was a world where one might simply drop in on people, to their delight. It's a more hurried world now and apparently a less personal one. But these changes make intentional efforts for relationship more significant than ever. Congregation-wide email announcements are a wonderful administrative aid, but personal email notes at appropriate times are pastoral, and a handwritten note can be nearly priceless. The business world is now skilled at phony intimacy; all of us receive solicitation letters that call us by our first name as if we were old friends, or at least members of the same club. In a culture of make-believe caring, pastors are a reality by nature of their office—but only if we take the time to use it. And, please God, only if it is sincere. Nothing is more off-putting than intimacy that is patronizing or used for effect. *Friendship* and *caring* are high-value words, thus they are words the unscrupulous try to counterfeit.

It's easy for the pastor to forget this hidden power, a power that for centuries has resided in the caring pastor or priest more than in any other profession or position. According to surveys, however, this standing is currently in decline. While secular merchandising searches for ways to convince the populace that they are known personally, pastors pursue more ways to be "efficient," which is a proper role in its own right, but not when it also makes us more distant. Some pastors are like the tragic character in Russell Conwell's epic lecture "Acres of Diamonds": they go around the world (in professional literature and conferences) to find ways to be more effective, not knowing that the treasure is in their own backyard.[3] Just as Conwell's hero spent his life looking for something that was in his own yard, we pastors search for treasures of effectiveness while ignoring the genius of intimacy that comes with our daily function as pastor and friend. Many commercial bodies try to convince their clients that they care. We have a head start toward this perception, and it is tragic if we forfeit it.

The Sermon Has Heart

It's not by chance that the preacher's daily attitude toward people and his or her relationship with them affect the sermon itself. In some ways the effect is subtle, but it is also logical. Preaching is a relationship: it is one person talking with another. This is one of the most personal relationships in which we humans can engage. This is especially true if the preacher is a good listener—and remember, there can't be good conversation without good listening. This relationship begins in day-by-day connections with the people. There's an old formula from a former world of pastoral preaching: "You can't preach a sermon under twenty calls a week." That is, a pastor must be concerned not only with hours spent in study (a rule also honored more in theory than in practice) but also with hours spent in firsthand communication with people.

Sometimes these hours feed directly into the sermon-making process in that they show the preacher the joys, sorrows, hopes, despairs, laughter and tears with which people are living. This comes in hospital calls and periods of counseling, but also in the simple stuff of daily conversation, including the chitchat that is of little obvious significance but that often holds more substantial discourse together. That is, "quality time" requires time if there is to be quality time. It can appear in the midst of incidental time. Sometimes when we think we're only shepherds on the hillside, angels quietly appear. Don't try to make every conversation into big business; to do so is to make an object out of the other person. But don't be surprised when big things happen in the midst of little business, and be ready for it. I confess with regret that I sometimes missed it.

The preacher needs to know the eternal quality that inhabits every day. This knowledge is both compelling and freeing. If we know that every day is composed of the stuff of eternity, we will treat each day with awe and excitement. We will remind ourselves that only God can know how far-reaching any event on any day may prove to be: how a friendly wave in the midst of a traffic jam may quiet a harried driver who otherwise would that evening speak a damning word to spouse or child, helping evil spiral on in ever-widening circles. A generous soul not only gives a dollar to the panhandler, he also chats with him for a moment, making him a human being rather than an object of charity. Life becomes big and very exciting when we know we live and speak and dream on the outskirts of eternity.

When we live with this eternal sense, we also gain an unlikely freedom. We realize that we are not alone in this daily amalgam and that God is with us not only to make our best deeds far-reaching but also to redeem and correct our errors, misjudgments and flat-out sins. The preacher should know this better than anyone and should convey this sense of eternal centeredness to all who meet him or her.

This knowledge must infuse the pastor's study, especially in the process of sermon preparation. That is, the pastor must sense that a person is looking over her shoulder as she writes or sitting across the room in conversation. We are doing more than looking for another illustration, another quote, a further insight on a difficult biblical passage. We are preparing to deliver an eternal word to eternal people. And it must, therefore, come from the heart.

We are unique in this assignment. Mind you, I feel repeatedly when I'm reading the best of the poets or novelists or playwrights that they often look very deep into the human soul. When the wife of Willy Loman appeals on behalf of her less-than-noble husband, "Attention must be paid," I know that the playwright sees the value of a human being. I don't know what Arthur Miller believed about God or the soul, but I confess with sorrow that I wish some sermons evoked as deep a sense of human pathos. Sometimes I think the nominally irreligious poet or novelist is more sensitive to the struggles of the human soul simply because he or she writes without hope—and then I feel uneasy about the kind of preaching that treats issues superficially.

For one, we can miss the grandeur and nobility resident in every human being. We preachers need to remember the eternal quality of the people to whom we preach: that the breath of God resides in them and that their original address is Eden. Then we need to know how lost we are and to understand that it is just as bad to be lost on Wall Street or in a suburban home as it is to be lost on skid row. And then we must remember the incomparable good news of salvation in Christ, which is life eternal—all of which reminds us that we preachers work with a total human biography that contemporary novelists and playwrights rarely approach. Who will do it if we don't?

The seventeenth-century English preacher Richard Baxter vowed that he wanted to preach "as never sure to preach again, / And as a dying soul to dying men." Something of that quality of mind should center the preacher's mind during sermon preparation. But how exactly does that mood fit with announcing the annual church picnic and with a Sunday sermon on a relatively pedestrian theme? Again, the preacher must know both the levity and the gravity of the gospel. We deliver good news in the midst of the bad news of the daily culture. We deliver a faith that brings joy to the world. No one is better equipped to laugh and to laugh deeply and fully than those who believe that God lives and reigns. To be serious is not the same thing as to be morbid. The people at Lazarus's tomb were struck by Jesus' tears because they had so often seen him laugh at festive dinners.

Know this for sure: that the sermon that unfolds in the preacher's study had better interest the preacher. We can hardly expect a sermon to hold the attention of listeners (or readers) if it hasn't held the attention of the preacher during the creative process. The sermon must be a live and lively thing in the preacher's soul if it is to compete with the distractions that solicit the attention of the people who sit in chairs and pews on any weekend.

Passion in Delivery

It's when the preacher sets out to deliver the sermon that distractions are most disheartening. Some of these distractions are as old as the night when Eutychus fell out of his window seat "as Paul talked on and on" (Acts 20:9). This reminds us that weariness or boredom is traditionally among the worst of distractions. And there's coughing in the congregation: it seems to come just when you're speaking the key word in the sentence. And there are people who slip out and return, and infants who cry or entice adults to entertain them, and teenagers who major in boredom, and cell phones that go off, and individuals who decide to communicate via Twitter. What fighting chance does a sermon have?

Some preachers and counselors to preachers see the answer in the use of video clips and sermon aids on a screen or in a bulletin insert. I won't venture into such because my chapter title speaks of the preacher's secret resources—that is, resources not common to the secular culture. Besides, one of the preacher's best resources is the innate intimacy of person speaking to person, and it's quite possible that the image on the screen or the urging to fill in outline blanks distracts from that intimacy. There is an immediacy in the person standing in living presence. We should be sure when we introduce distance into the preacher's relationship that the gain is commensurate.

There is a special power in the passion of the preacher. Some weeks ago I worshiped in a church where one of my former students was preaching. He was never one of my most polished speakers, either in uniqueness of material or in style of delivery, but he is building a vital, earnest body of believers. I saw why. It was clear that the sermon mattered to this young man, and as such the sermon was persuasive. He delivered it not because it was in the lectionary and not because he thought it was an interesting idea, but because in some measure he felt compelled to say it. He thought it mattered. He thought the people mattered, and God mattered, and eternity mattered.

The secular, profane world uses a phrase that is more theological than they realize. They speak of someone "giving a damn" about what they're saying. Our calling to preach is one that could use that term theologically. It is what Richard Baxter was saying in more conventional ways when he described himself as "a dying soul preaching to dying men." The preacher cares, cares profoundly, cares eternally, and out of this caring comes passion in delivery. The person in the pew is not a prospect to be sold, a case to be closed, a vote to be won; the person in the pew is a human being for whom Christ died, a human being living in the poverty of the prodigal in the pigsty while there is food in the Father's house. The preacher who knows this and who can remember it when the same old people seem to have the same old facial expression has a secret resource that the secular culture could rightly envy.

In the mid-1920s—when radio, the first insistent distraction, was still a novelty and when motion pictures became "talking pictures"— one of the nation's foremost preachers, Ralph W. Sockman, diagnosed preaching's problem in a lecture for religious professionals. "There is no life-and-death urgency about [some preaching]," Sockman said. "The sense of sin is not poignant because[f] the old vivid personal relationships fade in the mind of the man who thinks in terms of universal spirit, natural law, and divine energy. God becomes merely 'man's giant shadow hailed divine.'"[4] More recently a seminary professor of homiletics said it again, perhaps still more forcefully: "One thing we are waiting for is for preachers who feel the strong wind, who sense the heights above them and the abyss below and take a deep breath and preach a life-changing gospel."[5] That kind of passion cuts through distractions.

This kind of counsel is not for the faint of heart or the gospel equivalent of the summer patriot. I'm speaking of something we preachers cannot buy in the Internet's collection of illustrative material or at next season's professional conference. Mind you, there is much to be learned. But most of our best resources are those that have been part of our calling since the prophets and poets of the Hebrew Scriptures. We need to have the character to become newly acquainted with God, with the people to whom we minister and with our own wandering souls.

The Witness in the Pews

Nearly all pastors have a resource in the pews that goes unused. It is the witness of what secular culture calls "the satisfied customer." Churches of several denominations celebrate "Laymen's Sunday," in which lay people lead in prayer, read the Scripture and preach. More often than not the sermon is a report on the person's spiritual journey, and nearly always it is moving and convincing. Some apologize that nothing "big" has happened in their life, yet there is a persuasive authenticity in what they say.

This resource deserves more than annual use. One of the greatest strengths of Alcoholics Anonymous is that part of the meeting where some typical Joe or Jane stands up and says, "I'm Joe R. I'm an alcoholic. Today I'm celebrating four years, three months and eighteen days of sobriety." This statement can evoke a response from those gathered that would fit a back-country revival meeting. The newcomer tells herself that maybe this would work for her too, and yet another AA member draws strength for his own journey.

The "prayer and praise" portion of the Sunday evening services of my childhood included time for testimonies. There was seldom a particularly remarkable one. Some were quite predictable: I knew what Brother Allen or Sister Green would say before they started. But those witnesses helped me to a conviction that I've never lost: that the gospel of Christ changes lives, and more than that, that this change is an unpredictable but continuing process. I realize now that in those testimonies I was getting a current *Pilgrim's Progress*.

Many churches call on laypeople to give a personal appeal during a financial campaign, but this is a limited and somewhat digressive role, as if a layperson's only role in the church were money. Every faith journey is its own kind of miracle. It is wonderful, yes, that someone has been saved from drugs or crime. But it is just as wonderful when one has been saved from prideful arrogance, or from overweening loneliness, or from despair that used to make every day a torture. I sometimes wish that our churches had the kind of AA atmosphere where I could stand up and say, "I'm Ellsworth K, and I'm a sinner. But I've now been following Christ for (blank) years. Not perfectly, I confess. But I'm still following on, and glad of it."

I daresay that one of the best-kept secrets in many churches is the company of people who have a faith story to tell—and who rarely tell it. In early Methodism this happened in the class meetings. Today, larger churches could make this a grace-filled feature in a Sunday class or a study group. And sometimes, yes, on Sunday morning. Probably not by open mike, but by the pastor's selection and with his or her careful explanation. It can be somebody's story of how they survived a bereavement, or dealt with the loss of a job, or made progress in coping with a certain besetting sin. And particularly, about how they came to Christ and Christ to them.

"But what if the person later fails?" someone asks. I sympathize with the question. Alcoholics Anonymous deals often with this issue. And its response is that it doesn't incite judgmentalism or defeat in fellow members but compassion, prayer and the extending of friendship. It would remind our middle class Christians that Christianity isn't easy. It's tougher than a club because it's eternal business.

Go for It!

There's more to be said. Every day I see new examples of the world of distraction and ponder new ways to preach in such a culture. I hope that I have set your own mind and soul to thinking, so that you can go further on your own. But never forget that eternity and the big issues are on our side. So, too, is the one who knows the human mind and soul most intimately—the Holy Spirit. The secular experts would sell their souls to get the resources that come to us with our calling.

ACKNOWLEDGMENTS

Scholars often express their gratitude to research specialists who have helped them through the maze of one or more of the world's great libraries. I choose to give belated thanks to librarians who allowed a sixteen-year-old to wander in the religion section of the public library in Sioux City, Iowa, a very long time ago. One of those days I came upon Henry Van Dyke's Beecher Lectures, *The Gospel for an Age of Doubt*. Among other things Beecher's book made me realize that while humans are always the same, they are also always influenced in some measure by the temper of their times. So it is that in the past several years, I began pondering the problems and opportunities we preachers and teachers face in what I see as an Age of Distraction. In a very real sense this book began in the stacks of a modest Midwestern public library.

I am grateful, too, to my students at Asbury Theological Seminary, whose desire to be better preachers continually inspires me to be a more effective teacher of preaching. I am grateful always to my wife, Janet, who is untiringly faithful in her enthusiasm for all that I do—teaching, preaching, writing, living.

Al Hsu, senior editor at InterVarsity Press, has been gracious and helpful beyond my expectations since our first correspondence. Any unfortunate lapses in this book are mine; they surely are not for lack of editorial attention. I'm also grateful to the two outside editorial consultants whose candid, anonymous evaluations were exceedingly helpful. They blessed me with an unintentional benefit. One reader described a particular chapter as "the worst of the book," and recommended that I replace it. The other reader called the same chapter "Great. I have most of the chapter marked as excellent." I've known the same variety of after-service comment as a preacher, but never in writing and never from such qualified judges.

I am especially grateful to the eleven people who contributed sidebars. They made their observations after reading the first chapter and attempting from that to sense what the entire book would be. I cherish their insights and anticipate that readers will find the sidebars stimulating.

We preachers are a special lot. Next to my salvation I consider this calling the greatest privilege of my life. Yes, if I could, I would do it again. And again. And again. Thus I hope dearly that my colleagues in preaching and teaching will find help in what I have written.

J. Ellsworth Kalas

NOTES

Chapter 1

[1]Douglas Quenqua, "Cellphone Talkers Proved To Be Irritants, Study Says," *The New York Times*, March 14, 2013, p. A19.

Chapter 2

[1]Barry Schwartz, *The Paradox of Choice* (New York: HarperCollins, 2004), pp. 9-10.
[2]Fleming Rutledge, *And God Spoke to Abraham* (Grand Rapids: Eerdmans, 2011), p. 267.
[3]Matthew Sleeth, *24/6* (Carol Stream, IL: Tyndale, 2012), pp. 6-7.
[4]Kathleen Norris, *Acedia and Me* (New York: Riverhead, 2008), p. 102.

Chapter 3

[1]G. A. Studdert-Kennedy, "Temptation," *The Best of G. A. Studdert-Kennedy* (London: Hodder & Stoughton, 1947), p. 210.
[2]National Public Radio, Oct. 15, 2012.
[3]Leon R. Kass, *The Beginning of Wisdom* (Chicago: University of Chicago Press, 2003), p. 1.
[4]G. K. Chesterton, in *The Oxford Dictionary of Quotations*, ed. Elizabeth Knowles (New York: Oxford University Press, 2004), p. 217.
[5]Cynthia Ozick, *The Din in the Head* (Boston: Houghton Mifflin, 2006), pp. 157-62.
[6]Charles Jefferson, "The Narrowness of Jesus," in *20 Centuries of Great Preaching* 7 (Waco, TX: Word, 1971), p. 69.
[7]Leon Botstein, "An Opening That Echoes Endlessly," *The Wall Street Journal*, December 22-23, 2012, p. C-9.
[8]George H. Morrison, *Meditations on the Gospels* (Chattanooga, TN: AMG, 1996), back jacket leaf.
[9]George H. Morrison, *Morning Sermons* (New York: Fleming H. Revell, 1932), p. viii.
[10]Jefferson, "Narrowness," p. 46.

Chapter 4

[1]Peter J. Gomes, *The Good Life* (New York: HarperOne, 2003), p. 121.

[2]Barry Schwartz, *The Paradox of Choice* (New York: HarperCollins, 2004), p. 106.

[3]Ibid., pp. 106-7.

[4]Eugene H. Peterson, *The Pastor* (New York: HarperOne, 2011), p. 104.

[5]Larry Whitham, *A City Upon a Hill* (New York: HarperOne, 2007), p. 23.

[6]Augustine of Hippo, *Confessions*, 1.1.

Chapter 5

[1]"Streep and Jones," *AARP The Magazine*, August-September 2012, p. 84.

[2]Jon Sweeney, *Daily Guideposts 2012* (New York: Guideposts, 2012), p. 276.

[3]Kevin Belmonte, *A Year with G. K. Chesterton* (Nashville: Thomas Nelson, 2012), pp. 11-12.

[4]I have become fond of the works of Kilian McDonnell, a Benedictine monk and scholar who began writing poetry in his late seventies. He has a gift for poems about Bible passages and personalities, giving what could be whole sermons in a dozen or twenty lines. And he has a sense of humor, which is a great gift for any communicator.

Chapter 6

[1]Peter J. Gomes, *The Good Life* (New York: HarperOne, 2003), pp. 168-69.

[2]Ross Douthat, *Bad Religion: How We Became a Nation of Heretics* (New York: Free Press, 2012), p. 233.

[3]"A Psalm of Life," in Henry Wadsworth Longfellow, *The Complete Poetical Works of Longfellow* (Boston: Houghton Mifflin, 1893).

[4]Fleming Rutledge, *And God Spoke to Abraham* (Grand Rapids: Eerdmans, 2011), p. 366.

[5]Oscar Sherwin, *John Wesley, Friend of the People* (New York: Twayne, 1961), pp. 145-46.

[6]Quoted in Sherwin, *John Wesley*, p. 146.

[7]Blaise Pascal, *Pensées*, 170.

Chapter 7

[1]Eugene H. Peterson, *The Pastor* (New York: HarperOne, 2011), p. 135.

[2]James Rhem, "The Way He Sees It," *On Wisconsin*, Summer 2000, p. 12.

[3]John Donne, "A Hymn to God the Father."

[4]I suggest Epstein's collected essays, *Narcissus Leaves the Pool*, or his book-length study, *Snobbery, the American Version*.

Chapter 8

[1]When I observed that surely there's a restaurant somewhere called "The Oaks of Mamre," a friendly editor discovered that there is such in Indianapolis, and also a farm in Texas.

[2]Alexander Pope, "An Essay on Criticism," 1711.

Chapter 9

[1]David Brooks, "Changes words reveal: 'evil' is out, 'self' is in," *Lexington (KY) Herald-Leader,* May 28, 2013, p. A-9.

[2]In Lady Holland, *A Memoir of the Reverend Sydney Smith,* 1855.

[3]Jonathan Swift, *The Works of Dr. Jonathan Swift, Volume IV,* Edinburgh, 1761, p. 390.

[4]Ralph Waldo Emerson, *Self-Reliance and Other Essays,* 1841.

[5]Margaret Pepper, *The Harper Religious and Inspirational Quotation Companion* (New York: Harper & Row, 1989), p. 334.

[6]Eric Metaxas, *Bonhoeffer: Pastor, Martyr, Prophet, Spy* (Nashville: Thomas Nelson, 2010), p. 106.

[7]Fleming Rutledge, *And God Spoke to Abraham* (Grand Rapids: Eerdmans, 2011), p. 251.

[8]Isaac Bashevis Singer, "Genesis," in *Congregation,* ed. David Rosenberg (New York: Harcourt Brace Jovanovich, 1987), p. 8.

Chapter 10

[1]In this instance I'm using the word *spiritual* as in common secular parlance, such as the "spirituality" section of a bookstore, which may have little to do with spirituality as a Christian sees it.

[2]Janet Maslin, "Out of Time: The Sins of Immediacy," *The New York Times,* March 14, 2013, p. C4.

[3]Russell H. Conwell, *Acres of Diamonds* (New York: Harper Brothers, 1915).

[4]Ralph W. Sockman, *Men of the Mysteries* (New York: Abingdon, 1927), p. 65.

[5]Thomas G. Long, "Why Sermons Bore Us," *Christian Century,* September 6, 2011, p. 31.

IVP PRAXIS
EQUIPPING LEADERS FOR MINISTRY

"...TO EQUIP HIS PEOPLE FOR WORKS OF SERVICE,
SO THAT THE BODY OF CHRIST MAY BE BUILT UP."

EPHESIANS 4:12

God has called us to ministry. But it's not enough to have a vision for ministry if you don't have the practical skills for it. Nor is it enough to do the work of ministry if what you do is headed in the wrong direction. We need both vision *and* expertise for effective ministry. We need *praxis*.

Praxis puts theory into practice. It brings cutting-edge ministry expertise from visionary practitioners. You'll find sound biblical and theological foundations for ministry in the real world, with concrete examples for effective action and pastoral ministry. Praxis books are more than the "how to" – they're also the "why to." And because *being* is every bit as important as *doing*, Praxis attends to the inner life of the leader as well as the outer work of ministry. Feed your soul, and feed your ministry.

If you are called to ministry, you know you can't do it on your own. Let Praxis provide the companions you need to equip God's people for life in the kingdom.

www.ivpress.com/praxis